RESEARCHING SPECIAL & INCLUSIVE EDUCATION

RESEARCHING SPECIAL & INCLUSIVE EDUCATION

KERRY VINCENT
HELEN BENSTEAD

Los Angeles | London | New Delhi
Singapore | Washington DC | Melbourne

Los Angeles | London | New Delhi
Singapore | Washington DC | Melbourne

SAGE Publications Ltd
1 Oliver's Yard
55 City Road
London EC1Y 1SP

SAGE Publications Inc.
2455 Teller Road
Thousand Oaks, California 91320

SAGE Publications India Pvt Ltd
B 1/I 1 Mohan Cooperative Industrial Area
Mathura Road
New Delhi 110 044

SAGE Publications Asia-Pacific Pte Ltd
3 Church Street
#10-04 Samsung Hub
Singapore 049483

Editor: Delayna Spencer
Assistant editor: Catriona McMullen
Production editor: Sarah Sewell
Copyeditor: William Baginsky
Proofreader: Clare Weaver
Marketing manager: Lorna Patkai
Cover design: Wendy Scott
Typeset by: C&M Digitals (P) Ltd, Chennai, India
Printed in the UK

Library of Congress Control Number: 2021950654

British Library Cataloguing in Publication data

A catalogue record for this book is available from the British Library

ISBN 978-1-5297-0908-7
ISBN 978-1-5297-0907-0 (pbk)

At SAGE we take sustainability seriously. Most of our products are printed in the UK using responsibly sourced papers and boards. When we print overseas we ensure sustainable papers are used as measured by the PREPS grading system. We undertake an annual audit to monitor our sustainability.

CONTENTS

Contents

LIST OF ABBREVIATIONS

AAI	Animal-assisted interaction
AEI	Australian Education Index
ALSPAC	Avon Longitudinal Study of Parents and Children
ASD	Autism spectrum disorder
BEI	British Education Index
BERA	British Educational Research Association
BSL	British Sign Language
CAQDAS	Computer-aided qualitative data analysis software
DCD	Developmental coordination disorder
DfE	Department for Education
ERIC	Education Resources Information Centre
FASD	Fetal alcohol spectrum disorder
GCSE	General Certificate of Secondary Education
HLTA	Higher level teaching assistant
IEP	Individual education plan
IPA	Interpretive phenomenological analysis
MMR	Measles, mumps and rubella (vaccination)
NGOs	Non-governmental organisations
SEND	Special educational needs and/or disability
SPSS	Statistical Package for the Social Sciences
TA	Teaching assistant
UK	United Kingdom
UNCRC	United Nations Convention on the Rights of the Child

LIST OF FIGURES

LIST OF TABLES

ABOUT THE AUTHORS

Dr Kerry Vincent

Kerry is a senior lecturer in Inclusive Education at the University of Canterbury (NZ) and has a particular interest in learner 'differences' and how these are conceptualised and responded to within schools. In the past, she has worked as a teacher, educational psychologist and researcher. Her interest in inclusive education was sparked in her second year of teaching when she unexpectedly found herself the teacher of a profoundly deaf child. She learned, often through trial and error, that the best outcomes occurred when she focused not on learner 'differences' but rather on how to modify the educational environment in ways that would support children's learning and well-being. She also learned that children and young people have valuable insights to contribute to our understandings of them, if only we take the time and find the means to truly listen to what they have to say. It is this view that underpins this book.

Dr Helen Benstead

Helen is a senior lecturer in the School of Education at the University of Sunderland and is programme leader of the MA in Special Educational Needs, Disability and Inclusion. Helen has considerable experience in the teaching of research methods in education and supervision of research in this field, with a specific interest in innovative methodologies to support and enable the participation of a range of children and adults with additional needs. Helen has published widely on the role of teaching assistants and their impact on the social inclusion of pupils identified with SEND. Helen has worked in central and local government, as a policy maker/advisor on Education and Youth at Mayor of London and within the Cabinet Office, and ran a social enterprise supporting teaching assistants in schools across the country, from 2015 to 2022.

ACKNOWLEDGEMENTS

We are grateful to all of our students, past and present, whose experiences of our programmes have formed the basis of this book. Your suggestions and contributions to teaching and learning in special and inclusive education have been invaluable in steering the direction of our writing and providing an effective focus for our work. We feel especially privileged to work alongside students on their research journeys in this field and hope that our book serves as a source of inspiration and support through the research journeys to come.

We are also grateful to the Sage team for their support, positivity and responsiveness through our writing journey. Our special thanks go to Cat and Delayna for matching us as writers and for being so amenable to our suggestions for change as the book evolved.

Kerry's acknowledgements

My grateful thanks go to my sister Nicola Cassie for her careful proofreading of chapters and also to good friend Jeanelle De Gruchy who encouraged me to 'go for it' when I was initially hesitant to take on this extended writing project in the midst of a major relocation.

Helen's acknowledgements

Thanks to my husband Richard, whose Saturday morning walks with our baby son George allowed me to write this book during my maternity leave. I will be forever grateful for your supportiveness and encouragement. To my father Alan, thank you for your expert proofreading skills.

1
INTRODUCTION

━━━━━━━━ **Chapter objectives** ━━━━━━━━

By the end of this chapter you will:

- ✓ Have considered what is meant by the term 'research' and what differentiates research from more general 'finding out' activities
- ✓ Recognise that you already have some research knowledge and skills
- ✓ Know why this book was written, who it is for and what readers will gain from it
- ✓ Understand why we advocate an approach to research that endeavours to include the voices and experiences of children and young people with SEND
- ✓ Know something about what each subsequent chapter will provide

This introductory chapter aims to start you thinking about research as a concept and to demystify any ideas you may have about research as something that is undertaken only by academic experts. We explain why we think that research in special and inclusive education is important and we clarify our understandings of some of the fundamental concepts that we refer to throughout the book. Towards the end of the chapter we set out the key purposes of the book and provide an overview of its structure and content.

Activity 1.1

What is research?

Before reading on, stop and think about your current understandings about research. Use the three questions below to prompt your thinking.

1 What do you understand by the term research? (What images and words come to mind when you say the word? In what ways is research different from something that would not be classified as research?)
2 Why is research important? (How do schools/society/children and young people benefit from research?)
3 What do you think makes the difference between 'good' and 'poor' research?

Defining research

The word 'research' is said to derive from the sixteenth-century French word *rechercher* (to find, seek, search for), and prior to that, the Latin *circare* (to go around, to wander). These etymological roots still have much in common with our understandings of research today. Research is about seeking answers but the process, even when carefully planned, is often not straightforward and may involve some 'going around'. In our experience, it is best to expect the unexpected when undertaking research, both in terms of the practical organisation of a project, and what is revealed through research findings. Research is like an adventure in that the outcomes cannot be known in advance. That, of course, is exactly why we do it: to learn something that we did not know beforehand. This is what makes research both challenging and exciting.

Box 1.1 presents four different definitions of research taken from popular educational research texts. Each is different but you can see some common themes. It is the purposeful and systematic elements that differentiate research from more general 'finding out' activities.

Box 1.1

Some definitions of research

'Research is purposeful investigation, aimed at finding out things we did not know before' (Lambert, 2012: 12).

'Research is a purposeful and systematic activity designed to answer questions, solve problems, illuminate situations and add to our knowledge' (Mutch, 2013: 30).

'Research is best conceived as the process of arriving at dependable solutions to problems through the planned and systematic collection, analysis, and interpretation of data' (Mouly, 1978: 16).

'A research project, whatever its size and complexity, consists of defining some kind of research problem, working out how this problem can be investigated, doing the investigation work, coming to conclusions on the basis of what one has found out, and then reporting the outcome' (Walliman, 2006: 29).

You might think of research as being something you have not done before or something about which you know very little, but many of us have undertaken or been part of research without realising it. For example, many readers of this book will be students. Before you began your studies, you will have made some decisions that have important implications for your future lives and careers. Which programme of study interests me? Which universities offer that programme? Which of those universities is going to be the best for me? The chances are that you did not simply select a course or a university at random but, rather, took a more systematic approach that involved gathering a range of information from a range of different sources. Perhaps you went online and looked at different university prospectuses to see which institutions offered what you were interested in. You may have attended open days or made direct enquiries to staff at specific institutions. You may have sought the opinions of people you know who have attended a particular university or programme of study. You may have looked at university rankings such as those produced by the annual National Student Survey or the Teaching Excellence Framework in the UK. In other words, you started with a particular aim or purpose (your research question) and sought out a range of information relevant to that question (gathered your data). Then you would have reviewed all of the information you had gathered (analysed your data) and made a decision based on the evidence (come to a conclusion).

Similarly, you will almost certainly have contributed to someone else's research. Most of us, at some point, will have completed a questionnaire or interview, either face to face, over the phone or via the internet. A common example is when we are asked to engage in some market research about a particular product, service or company. In other words, research is not something that is undertaken only by academics or professionals who are considered experts in their field (Robert-Holmes, 2011). Rather it is something that is going on around us all the time, and also something that can be undertaken by anyone once they have acquired the necessary knowledge, understanding and skills.

Activity 1.2

'Everyday' research

Think of an everyday activity or decision that required you to use some research skills in order to make an informed decision – for example, what brand and model of smartphone or tablet to buy, which job to apply for, where to go on holiday and what travel and accommodation arrangements will allow you to stay within your given budget.

1   Write the activity/decision at the top of a sheet of paper.
2   Compose a list of all the different actions you took to help you make an informed decision.
3   Reflect on which actions were more helpful than others in supporting evidence-based decisions. For example, were some sources of information more reliable than others?

Educational research can take many forms and explore a wide range of issues. It may be small scale, involving just a few people or contexts or large scale, involving many hundreds of people and taking place across multiple contexts. Similarly, it may employ just a single method of collecting and analysing data or multiple methods. For the purposes of this book, we view educational research as a process of purposeful exploration and discovery. It refers to a set of activities that aim to find something out about a specific issue, topic or question and results in conclusions which are based on evidence that has been systematically gathered and analysed (Mutch, 2013). In the context of special and inclusive education, we believe that research should be primarily about deepening understandings about professional concerns and interests in ways that contribute to improved practices and outcomes for children and young people, particularly those with special educational needs and disabilities (SEND).

Why undertake a research project in special needs and inclusion?

While the specific time frames, policies and practices differ from country to country, the education of children and young people with SEND around the world reflects similar patterns. In the past, many of these children were considered 'ineducable' and denied access to education altogether (Hodkinson, 2015). However, as education became more widely recognised as a human right, children and young people with disabilities in many countries have been able to access education, albeit largely in specialist, segregated settings. Although segregated education remains the case for some learners, many are now educated in mainstream settings in their local neighbourhoods. This means that working with learners with a range of SEND is an everyday reality for many more educational practitioners than in the past. Consequently, having the knowledge and skills to work effectively with an increasingly diverse student population is now an educational imperative. We believe that research in this area is particularly relevant to education students and practitioners today because not only does it have the potential to increase your own knowledge and understanding but it also contributes to the knowledge and understanding of others, and in this way leads to better practices and outcomes for learners with SEND.

This book aims not only to promote research in special needs and inclusive education but also to promote a particular approach to research in this area, one that takes into account the views and experiences of learners with SEND themselves. There are several reasons why we believe this to be important.

The missing voice of children

First, although children have long been participants in educational research, much of this has been *on* or *about* rather than *with* children, and historically children's views and experiences have been either absent or marginalised within the research literature (Bourke et al., 2017; Harcourt and Einarsdóttir, 2011). Underpinned by ideas from developmental psychology, children have traditionally been viewed as physically, cognitively and emotionally undeveloped – or as Kellett (2005) puts it, 'adults in waiting'. This has led to them being considered too immature to participate in research in their own right. In other words, children have historically been considered either incapable of making a meaningful contribution to research (and therefore not worth listening to) or as vulnerable and therefore in need of protection (Harcourt, 2011).

More recently, however, the new sociologies of childhood provide a different conceptualisation whereby children are seen not only as experts on their own lives but also capable of understanding and meaningfully engaging in research (Clark and Moss, 2011). Additionally, ratification of the United Nations Convention on the Rights of the Child (UNCRC, 1989) by many countries around the world has done much to promote research *with* rather than *on* children. These factors have supported participatory approaches to research with children. However, children's views and experiences continue to be marginalised within educational research (Kellett, 2010; Murray, 2017).

The missing voice of disabled people

The same themes can be seen when looking at disability research. That is, much early research in the field of disability involved research *on* rather than *with* people with disabilities and their views and experiences were largely excluded. Kiernan (1999) points out that it was not until the 1980s that people with learning disabilities in the UK were even invited to share their views and experiences about services that they received.

This occurred for the same reasons as those noted above for children; people with disabilities were viewed as incapable of understanding and meaningfully taking part in research, vulnerable and thus in need of protection. This 'leave it to the experts' approach to research was also underpinned by deficit constructions of those with disabilities inherent in the medical model of disability and contributed to unhelpful and negative stereotypes about disabled people. As noted by Cuskelly:

> For a long time researchers working with individuals who have a disability, and with their families, took a pathological view and focused on what was wrong, deviant or deficient in those individuals and their families. (2005: 99)

Whilst the disability rights movement has done much to support more affirming and participatory research with those with disabilities, this has often not extended to children. In this respect, children with disabilities are doubly marginalised: first, on account of being children, and second, on account of being disabled. Some commentators argue that this is especially true for children with particular disabilities – namely, learning disabilities or autism spectrum disorders (ASD) (Boxall and Ralph, 2009; MacLeod et al., 2014; Scott-Barrett et al., 2019). In their systematic review of qualitative research that focused on the views of young people with ASD about their educational experiences, Fayette and Bond (2017) found an over-representation of higher-functioning young people with ASD and far fewer studies with those whose communication or learning difficulties were more severe. With regard to the under-representation of learners' perspectives in research on inclusive education more generally, Messiou's (2016) analysis of the 640 articles published in the *International Journal of Inclusive Education* over a ten-year period (2005–2015) found that participatory and collaborative approaches (research *with* rather than *on* children and young people), accounted for only 3 per cent (20) of the studies. These more recent studies confirm that the marginalisation of some learners within research continues to be a cause for concern.

Reasons for these missing voices

That the voices noted above are missing is perhaps not surprising given that research designed to incorporate more active participation of children and young people with SEND is more complicated and time-consuming. Gaining access and approval from gatekeepers, addressing ethical concerns and interpreting learner-generated data all become more challenging, particularly in the case of very young children or those with more severe learning, social or communication difficulties. As Wall (2017) points out, even when a questionnaire or interview has been tailored specifically to minimise barriers to participation, variations in maturity and developmental stage may still limit the meaningful participation of some children and young people.

Similarly, we speculate that even when there are no cognitive or social communication barriers to consider, the perspectives of children with other disabilities, such as those with hearing and visual impairments, have been neglected within mainstream research simply due to methods not adequately taking account of their unique communication requirements.

We believe there is therefore a need for more research that seeks the perspectives of all children and young people, including those with SEND and those who experience other forms of marginalisation within our education systems. This is important not just from a human rights perspective but also because of what we learn *from* and *about* these learners. As some academics have pointed out, the competencies of children (with and without SEND) are *different from* rather than *lesser than* those of adults (Kellett, 2005; Lomax, 2012). Their perspectives are therefore needed, alongside those of adults, for full and balanced understandings. Importantly, the insights they provide have the potential to better inform policies and practices.

Special needs, inclusion and social justice

Finally, research in this field is important not just for human rights reasons but also for those related to social justice. We know, for example, that the educational community still has much to learn about how best to promote the learning and well-being of children and young people with SEND. Learners labelled as having autistic spectrum disorder (ASD) or attention deficit hyperactivity disorder (ADHD) or dyslexia, or social emotional or mental health issues feature disproportionately in the school exclusion statistics and are under-represented among those who achieve highly at school – as are other groups of learners, such as pupils from some ethnic minority groups and those coming from families with lower incomes (DfE, 2019). It is only by continuing to engage with all stakeholder groups (parents, children and young people, teachers and other educational professionals, support services and policy makers) that we will attain the social justice goals to which inclusive educators aspire. Research has an essential role to play with regard to this.

Key concepts referred to in this book
What do we mean by inclusive education?

It is important that you understand what we mean when we use certain terms in this book. We start with the much-used term 'inclusive education'. First, we recognise that inclusive education is a fuzzy concept about which there is no single agreed definition or understanding (Messiou, 2016). Rather, it is something that is understood very differently by different people and across different contexts. This is what makes inclusive education a complex field within which views about what is 'right', or 'good', or 'just' are often contested. We accept that there are a wide range of educational, social and political issues that complicate a unified understanding of inclusive education and we anticipate that debates about exactly what educational inclusion looks like in practice will continue for some time.

For the purposes of this book, there are two additional points we wish to emphasise in relation to our understanding of this concept. First, we subscribe to Ainscow and Booth's (1998) view of inclusive education as an ongoing process rather than a state. It involves recognising diversity and difference in affirming ways and taking steps to ensure that every learner is receiving an education that is responsive to their needs (Carrington et al., 2016). We also agree with those who argue that moving in an inclusive direction requires focusing more on the attitudes, beliefs, skills and resources of those responsible for providing education and less on the individual characteristics of a given learner or group of learners (Carrington et al, 2016; Giangreco et al., 2010).

Second, we view inclusive education as a process aimed at ensuring the presence, participation and achievement of all learners. As argued by Ainscow and Booth:

> Inclusion and exclusion are as much about participation and marginalisation in relation to race, gender, sexuality, poverty and unemployment as they are about traditional special education concerns with students categorised as low in attainment, disabled or deviant in behaviour. (1998: 2)

A learner who is unable to meaningfully participate in the everyday life of a classroom because they are a recent immigrant and are not yet proficient in English is just as much at risk of experiencing exclusion as a child with a learning disability, a sensory impairment, or social and communication difficulties. Similarly, such a learner is more likely to be excluded from mainstream research.

Accordingly, the students whose projects we have supervised over the years have focused on a wide range of issues, groups and individuals. What they all had in common was that learner differences often resulted in stigma or marginalisation within our educational institutions. Examples include learners whose first language is not English, those who belong to ethnic and religious minorities, those who are refugees or asylum-seekers, those from Gypsy, Roma and Traveller communities, and those who identify as gender diverse. While many of the examples and case studies found in this book relate to learners with SEND, you will also find examples that align with this broader understanding of inclusive education.

What about inclusive research?

More recently, there has been a rise in the number of published examples of what is referred to as inclusive research. This aligns closely with what others refer to as participatory research. These terms have been applied both to research with children generally and to research with other marginalised groups such as those with disabilities. In relation to disability, de Bruin (2017) defines inclusive research as that which aims to be transformative, emancipatory or participatory and that achieving this requires collaboration *with*, and researching *alongside* rather than *on*, people with disabilities. She explains that participatory research aims to emphasise the insider voices that have traditionally been silenced in experimental research. However, as is the case with the term 'inclusive education', there is no single agreed definition of inclusive research and research practices reflect considerable variations in how participation is understood. This can range from research participants simply being asked about their views, to working with them as co-researchers who contribute to the research aims, design and findings (Bourke et al., 2017; Davis and Watson, 2017).

In her work on ethical research with children, Alderson (2005) illustrates this variation by outlining three main levels of child involvement in research.

1   *Children as unknowing objects*: Research where children are not asked for their consent and may not even be unaware that they are being researched
2   *Children as aware subjects*: Research where informed consent is sought but is otherwise planned and undertaken without any additional input from children
3   *Children as active participants*: Research where children willingly take part in research which has flexible goals and methods (adapted from Alderson, 2005: 29–30)

It is the last point which aligns most closely with current articulations of inclusive or participatory research and is an approach that we wish to support through this book.

What do we mean by special needs?

You will have noticed that we have used the acronym SEND to refer to special educational needs and disability. This aligns with current usage in the UK. According to the *Special Educational Needs and Disability Code of Practice* (DfE and DH, 2015), a child or young person is considered to have a learning difficulty or disability if he or she 'has significantly greater difficulty in learning than the majority of others the same age' or 'has a disability which prevents or hinders him or her from making use of facilities of a kind generally provided for others of the same age' (DfE and DH, 2015: 16). This document makes the point that although there is considerable overlap between learners identified as having special educational needs (SEN) and those with disabilities, not *all* learners with disabilities also have SEN. For example, a child who uses a wheelchair to aid mobility may have no additional learning needs and is therefore not considered to have SEN. The *Code of Practice* also draws attention to the learning needs of children and young people with special circumstances, such as those in social care, those receiving home or alternative education, those in youth custody and those with medical needs (some of whom attend hospital schools). A special educational need is therefore not limited just to those with an identified disability. Instead, the emphasis is placed on learning difficulty or need. The *Code of Practice* identifies four broad areas of need which we summarise in Table 1.1.

Table 1.1 Four areas of need identified in the SEND Code of Practice (DfE and DH, 2015)

Area of need	Learners that it applies to
Communication and interaction	Learners with a range of speech, language and communication difficulties as well as those with ASD
Cognition and learning	Learners with moderate learning difficulties (MLD), severe learning difficulties (SLD) and profound and multiple learning difficulties (PMLD), as well as those with specific learning difficulties such as dyslexia and dyspraxia
Social, emotional and mental health difficulties	Learners with a range of needs – e.g. those with anxiety or depression or who display behaviours that cause concern such as disruptive behaviour, self-harming, substance abuse or eating disorders
Sensory and/or physical needs	Learners with visual or hearing impairments and those with physical or mobility difficulties

Finally, we wish to highlight that terminology is constantly changing and varies across national contexts. We have noticed that in the UK, as well as in Australia and New Zealand, the term 'additional learning need' is sometimes used rather than 'special educational need'. It is possible that in a few years time the former will replace the latter.

A cautionary note about labels

Terminology can be a complex business and the labels we ascribe to learners who are different in some way can be both helpful and unhelpful. One point we wish to emphasise is that a label reveals little about the specific abilities or learning needs of the individual to which it is applied. In other words, those with special educational needs or disabilities are not a homogenous group. No two learners with ASD or Down's syndrome or dyslexia, or any other label that might be applied, are the same. It is therefore important not to make assumptions about a learner, based primarily on the label.

Who is this book for and what does it provide?

The book has been written to support both undergraduate and postgraduate students with an interest in special needs and inclusive education as well as practitioner researchers. It will also be of value to students in related disciplines, such as early childhood education, social work, and health and social care. It is aimed particularly at those who are required to undertake a research project as part of their studies or those seeking to understand or further develop practices in their own professional settings.

The respective chapters are based on our experiences of working with students and practitioner researchers and aim to address commonly occurring questions and issues that arose when they were planning and undertaking their projects. Our experience with a wide range of students suggests that specific guidance on the practicalities of undertaking research that involves children and young people identified with SEND is particularly valued. This book therefore aims to guide you through the research process using practical examples drawn from real situations we and and our students encountered.

There are some content areas that we have deliberately excluded as discrete foci in this book simply because coverage in relation to special needs and inclusion would not be sufficiently different from other commonly used research texts. This book therefore does not offer specific guidance on how to write a research proposal or how to write your thesis or dissertation. It also excludes content on scholarly skills such as academic writing and referencing. Additionally, the practical orientation of the book means that we do not offer in-depth coverage of the many philosophical debates relevant to inclusive education. The Recommended reading section at the end of the chapter includes some suggestions for coverage of these topics.

The overall aim of this book is to give students and practitioner researchers the confidence to be creative, flexible and innovative when it comes to planning and undertaking their research in special needs and inclusive education. We want readers to understand that there is no single best way to approach their research but rather, all research projects will have their strengths and limitations.

Additionally, throughout the book we want neither to simplify nor fail to acknowledge some of the tensions and complexities involved in undertaking research in this field. These are evident at every stage of the research process – from identifying a specific focus and formulating a research question, to gaining the necessary approval, consents and access to settings or participants, to deciding what data-gathering methods will be the most suitable to achieve the aims of the research, and on what basis rigour and trustworthiness will be established. Once data has been gathered, there are issues related to analysis and interpretation, what to do with research findings and who 'owns' them. For each step in the research process, this book aims to equip you to consider a range of research possibilities and to make a judgement based on a clear understanding of the relative merits and disadvantages of each of your research decisions, and to assess the merits of those taken in other research. In these ways, the book aims to produce reflexive, intentional researchers who have the knowledge, skills and understandings to undertake high-quality research in relation to their specific interests and concerns.

As noted earlier in this chapter, we are conscious that despite much rhetoric about the importance of listening to children, their views and perspectives remain marginalised within the wider research literature. This trend is even more pronounced for children and young people with SEND as there are often additional challenges in eliciting their views. We hope that one additional outcome of this book is that more students and practitioner researchers will be willing to tackle these challenges and, in doing so, give greater prominence to the perspectives of children and young people with SEND in the wider research literature.

Book structure and overview

The book comprises 11 chapters. This introductory chapter has reviewed what is meant by the term 'research' and has clarified who this book is for, what readers will gain from it, and why we think research in the field of special needs and inclusive education is important. In the next chapter, we introduce you to some common research philosophies and perspectives in educational research. It aims to help you understand that there are different approaches to research in education and that each is underpinned by different assumptions about 'truth' and 'knowledge'. We explain why understanding the 'ologies' is important in relation to reading other people's research as well as justifying and undertaking your own.

Chapter 3 turns to practical matters related to getting started on your research study in special needs and inclusive education. We consider how you might go about identifying a general area of interest and how to develop this into a focused and viable research plan. We highlight the importance of a clearly articulated research question that has associated aims and objectives as well as the need for early consideration of potential research participants and settings.

The following chapter on research ethics examines a range of philosophical and practical matters that need to be considered when researching special needs and inclusive education. We cover questions such as: What is meant by ethical research? What makes research ethical (or unethical)? What are some of the organisational ethical codes of practice relevant to research in special needs and inclusive education and what are their key purposes and principles? This chapter reiterates an important point made by other researchers, that ethics are intrinsic to every part of the research process (Alderson and Morrow, 2020).

Chapter 5 turns to the place of the literature review in research. We discuss the key purpose of the literature review and its importance in explaining and justifying your research focus. We introduce you to some different ways of approaching your literature review and some useful sources of literature when researching special needs and inclusive education. We discuss the value of being selective about what you read as well as how to approach your reading with a critical eye.

Chapter 6 introduces readers to some common practical approaches that can be taken across a range of research designs. We look in particular at case study, action research, ethnography and systematic literature reviews as different ways of approaching your research in special needs and inclusive education.

The next three chapters turn to matters of data collection. Chapters 7 and 8 present some different ways of looking and listening, focusing in particular on observation, interviews and questionnaires. We discuss when and why each method might be used as well as the potential pitfalls and how these might be overcome. We also consider how these methods might be adapted to accommodate children and young people with SEND. Chapter 9 discusses less traditional data-collection methods that are particularly useful when working with young children or those with diverse communication needs and preferences. We introduce readers to the Mosaic approach, visual methods, research conversations and transect walks.

The final two chapters focus on what to do with your data once you have collected it. Chapter 10 introduces you to some different ways of managing, analysing, interpreting and displaying your data as well as how you might go about drawing and evidencing conclusions. Chapter 11 turns to the question of what to do now that your study is finished. We encourage you to reflect both on what you have learned about the research process as well as what you have learned in relation to your specific research question. Particularly where there are some clear implications for practice, we discuss how you might approach disseminating your findings more widely so that others can benefit from your research.

Recommended reading

- Nind, M. and Vinha, H. (2012) *Doing Research Inclusively, Doing Research Well? Report of the Study: Quality and Capacity in Inclusive Research with People with Learning Disabilities.* ESRC and University of Southampton.

Outline: This publication illustrates how disabled people themselves were an integral part of planning and undertaking the research described. Although this publication focuses on adults with learning disabilities, it highlights practices that could be more widely applied to both children and those with a range of disabilities. The report is available at: www.southampton.ac.uk/assets/imported/transforms/content-block/UsefulDownloads_Download/97706C004C4F4E68A8B54DB90EE0977D/full_report_doing_research.pdf

- Nind, M. (2017) The practical wisdom of inclusive research. *Qualitative Research*, 17(3): 278–88.

Outline: This article describes how some UK academics worked with people with learning disabilities to address some of the challenges involved in researching *with* rather than *on* people with disabilities.

- Punch, K. (2000) *Developing Effective Research Proposals*. London: Sage.

Outline: As suggested in the title, this book provides detailed coverage of how to plan, structure and seek approval for your research proposal. This topic is not covered in our book.

2

PERSPECTIVES IN RESEARCH: UNDERSTANDING THE 'OLOGIES'

━━━━━━━━━━ Chapter objectives ━━━━━━━━━━

By the end of this chapter you will:

- ✓ Be able to define some common terminology in exploring researcher perspectives
- ✓ Understand the two main 'camps' of researcher position in educational research and the emergence of a 'third camp'
- ✓ Identify the links between researcher position and theories of learning
- ✓ Be able to identify your researcher position when conducting research in special and inclusive education, to support you with navigating the remainder of this book

Introduction

The aim of this chapter is to introduce the most common research philosophies and per-spectives of researchers in education. This chapter should support you, as a researcher, to understand your own perspectives on why research is important and what you value and believe about the way in which research should be conducted. This will then support you as you move through the remaining chapters in this book, as it will underpin all of the methodological decision-making when planning a study in special and inclusive education.

This chapter presents a range of complex-sounding terminology, which can take some time to familiarise yourself with. However, the approach in this chapter is not to shy away from presenting this range in complexity of terminology and, instead, to sim-plify it by highlighting the connections rather than exploring the concepts separately. The intention is that this chapter can be used to some extent as a glossary of terminol-ogy associated with research philosophies that you may come across in your studies of research methods in education.

Introducing the 'ologies': Ontology and epistemology

To conduct research well, you not only need to choose the most appropriate method-ology, you also need to ensure that you have carefully thought through the ways in which your views about what should be valued in research link with the methodol-ogy you have chosen to employ. According to Scotland (2012: 10), 'it is impossible to engage in any form of research without committing (often implicitly) to ontological and epistemological positions'. The methodological approaches and methods that you choose to employ should always complement your epistemological views. This process is reflected in Figure 2.1 and represents the process that we will follow in the way this book is ordered. Planning research follows a clear pathway of thinking, which we will support you to navigate in this book.

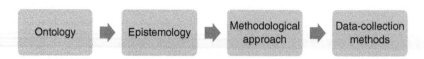

Figure 2.1   Thinking process for identifying paradigms

Definitions of key terms in this chapter
Ontology

The term ontology refers to the way in which we view the form and nature of the social world. It relates to the study of being, in the words of Scotland (2012) 'what is'. It is important for researchers to identify their own position on how the world works and what they believe about what can and cannot be explored via research. Once a researcher's ontological perspective is identified, the researcher is then in a position to explore their epistemological perspective.

Epistemology

As with ontology, epistemology is concerned with the way in which the world operates. However, it is more specifically concerned with the nature of knowledge. Researchers should explore their own assumptions about how knowledge can be created, acquired and communicated in order to best identify the most appropriate methodology to follow in their study. This is explained by Guba and Lincoln (1994: 108) in the question: what is the relationship between the would-be-knower and what can be known?

Methodological approach

This area of thinking refers specifically to the procedure or logic that will be followed in a given study. Both ontology and epistemology are integral to decision-making on the methodological approach selected, as the way in which an individual researcher views the nature of reality and the way in which knowledge is constructed will of course significantly inform the approach selected in a given study. The methodological approach is primarily concerned with the strategy of sampling participants and collecting data (Crotty, 1998). We will explore specific methodological approaches in much greater detail in Chapter 6.

Data-collection methods

Following on from determining the most appropriate methodological approach comes the choice of the most appropriate methods, which can be defined as the specific techniques and procedures used to collect data (Crotty, 1998). Data-collection methods in special and inclusive education studies often need careful adaptation to enable the participation of a variety of participants. We will explore a variety of effective ways of doing this in Chapters 7 to 9.

Note that there are two distinct types of data collection:

Qualitative: data that generally consists of words

Quantitative: data that generally consists of numbers

Paradigm

You will notice that the title of Figure 2.1 refers to paradigms. This is because the flow of thinking that we are leading you through, as a whole, is often termed a paradigm. Different paradigms are associated with different ontological and epistemological views – by extension, therefore, different methodological approaches and data-collection methods. It may be that a similar topic of research can be explored in very different ways, due to the researchers preferring different paradigms. Your past experiences will strongly shape the paradigm that you choose to align yourself with. There are many different paradigms, some of which are more commonly associated with conducting research in special and inclusive education. We will explore these paradigms across the remainder of this chapter.

Checkpoint 2.1

- The way in which we view the world, the nature of reality and the nature of knowledge have a strong influence over the approaches that we take as researchers.
- We need to spend some time exploring our own assumptions as practitioners to ensure that we are taking account of them when we're designing our methodology.
- The thought process we should follow results in identifying a particular paradigm that we can use to scaffold the remainder of the planning process for a piece of research.

Two 'camps' of researcher position

Researchers in education generally occupy one of two 'camps' in terms of their approach to research and in selecting the paradigm that they most closely associate themselves with. The presentation of these two 'camps' in this chapter involves significant generalisation, as the exploration of researcher positions is certainly more complex than these two camps may suggest. However, as many of you will be relatively new to research in education, it is helpful for you to use these two 'camps' as an introductory way to explore your personal positioning before you begin to plan your research project.

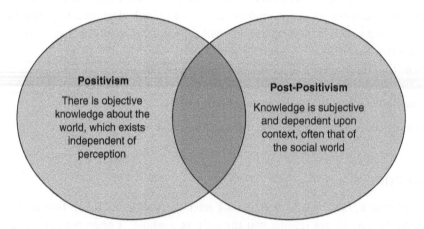

Figure 2.2   The two 'camps' of researcher position

Positivism

Historically, the majority of researchers in wider disciplines favoured research that involved quantitative (number-related) data, rather than qualitative (word-related) data. This position is often termed 'positivist' or 'realist.' In this view, researchers are often seeking objective truths (those that can be measured and can be used to create laws). They believe that objective truths exist independent of the researcher and that it is the role of the researcher to discover these truths. This perspective often most aligns itself with scientific enquiry and aims to quantify probabilities in relation to the topic of exploration. Therefore, researchers who hold a positivist view of the world generally implement solely quantitative data-collection methods and often aim to prove or disprove hypotheses. These researchers tend to align themselves with natural sciences and experimental research.

The theory of learning that most strongly aligns itself with a positivist paradigm could be argued to be that of behaviourism. The most notable academic linked to behaviourist research is B.F. Skinner, whose work aimed to identify cause-and-effect patterns, initially with animals and then relating to human behaviour. At a very basic level, in this theory of learning, repeated patterns of behaviour to certain stimuli can be extrapolated to develop laws and universal 'truths' about certain groups of people. Scientific experiments can be conducted to identify these patterns in behaviour to make generalisations about teaching and learning approaches in education more specifically. The relationships between specific variables are of paramount concern for the researcher and exist independent of the social context of the classroom. As individuals, positivists believe that we have no influence over 'what is', we are simply investigating and uncovering the meaning of 'what is'. So, educational researchers who follow a positivist approach often use quantitative data-collection methods that focus on collecting statistical data to reveal relationships – for example, closed-ended questionnaires and structured observations of behaviour.

Post-positivism

More recently, there has been a movement to value more than statistical relationships and quantitative data, particularly in educational research. It has been acknowledged that, although statistical relationships to determine cause and effect are important, this perspective alone fails to acknowledge the complexity of the variables at play in meaning-making. This movement is aligned with a post-positivist view of the world and often aligns with an interpretivist paradigm. Interpretivists believe that collecting quantitative data alone limits the understandings that researchers can develop. Although many post-positivists accept that objective truths can exist, they argue that what one person can view as an objective truth may be different from the next person. Thus, there is always an element of subjectivity in researchers' findings; the aim is to understand what meanings researchers give to realities, not to determine what the specifics of the realities are (Check and Schutt, 2012). In order to do this, most interpretivists elect to use qualitative data-collection methods, as they are aimed at understanding individuals' perspectives on the topic of interest. This approach is particularly common in modern educational research, due to the acknowledgement by many educational researchers that truths are difficult to ascertain without taking into account the research context – classrooms and socially complex concepts. Many believe that effective educational research takes account of this by implementing qualitative methods that can explore these complex social worlds.

The post-positivist and more specifically the interpretivist paradigms arguably have their roots in the theory of social constructivism. This perspective views dialogue as key to the meaning-making process; dialogue engenders higher-order thinking to promote learning that is not possible without collaborative intervention. The most influential figure in social constructivist theory is that of Lev Vygotsky (1978), whose work highlighted the perceived power of collaboration with a 'more knowledgeable other' in the enhancement of meaning-making and knowledge development. Fosnot (1989) specifically relates this concept to educational settings by describing the constructivist classroom as, 'a community of discourse engaged in activity, reflection and conversation' (p.34). It therefore follows that those of us who teach in classrooms that value discussion and collaboration are more likely to hold interpretivist viewpoints rather than those associated with positivism. We acknowledge that there is more to meaning-making than statistical relationships between variables; these relationships must be considered in context.

Activity 2.1

Determining your researcher position

Read the statements in Table 2.1 below and think about whether or not you agree with them. Then check the answers at the end of the chapter, which highlight whether the statements are more aligned with positivist/post-positivist positions. The position that you have the majority of statements in agreement with reflects your broad view.

Table 2.1 Activity: Positivism/post-positivism

Statement	Positivist/post-positivist?	Do you agree/disagree?
Everything can be measured, in one way or another, to identify patterns, causes and effects		
People's thoughts and behaviour can be measured statistically		
The only way to really understand the motivations behind people's actions is to talk to them about them		

Statement	Positivist/post-positivist?	Do you agree/disagree?
People can interpret things differently, and come to different conclusions, which means that it is impossible to reach objective truths		
People can interpret things differently, and come to different conclusions. All of these are valid, as there are different interpretations of reality		
Analysing academic results is the only way to make judgements on the efficacy of a school		
Unless statistics are involved in measuring something, our understandings can't be proven		
Children's behaviours can be predicted and measured		
Talking/discussion is vital to creating new knowledge		

The 'two camps' and research in special and inclusive education

When we relate the 'two camps' of research position to conducting research in special and inclusive education, there are many parallels with the interpretivist paradigm. At its heart, the principle of inclusion encourages us to view each individual as unique. We are therefore less likely to seek 'truths' that pertain to all individuals with special educational need. Instead, we are more likely to seek to understand the characteristics of individuals and small groups in context, to make more tentative generalisations about effective teaching and learning approaches. This means that we will often employ methodologies that take account of social interaction in the teaching and learning process. So, we often employ data-collection methods that involve some level of discussion/talk – for example, inter-viewing or observations of social interaction.

However, it is possible to undertake research in special and inclusive education align-ing with a positivist paradigm. The nature of the political landscape in education means that educators are required to develop policies and practices that work for populations. Educational policy is required to advocate certain approaches that work for all children in education systems, so as to allow for all students to access a basic level of education. In England, the *Special Educational Needs and Disability Code of Practice* (DfE and DH, 2015) is an example of this approach, as is the National Curriculum (DfE, 2014). Both of these policies are required to be relevant to all children accessing education. Therefore, the structure of our schooling system means that it is necessary to generate universal 'truths' or laws in education. This can be extended to educational research; because it is necessary to create an educational system that works for all, research that aims to develop generalisable 'truths' is a legitimate aim.

Very often, research in education that follows a positivist paradigm focuses on educational outcomes of the students in our education systems. All students undertake examinations or undergo formalised testing at some point in their educational career. Therefore, the opportunities to quantify success or failure in education systems are vast, and very much align with a positivist approach to research. Of course, this is more complex when we look at testing in the field of special and inclusive education because many individuals with complex special educational needs cannot access universal and traditional testing systems. It is therefore automatically more difficult to conduct research that aims to generate 'truths' in relation to academic outcomes in this field. Nevertheless, it is possible to conduct research in special and inclusive education that aims to identify cause-and-effect relationships to make generalisations about effective teaching and learning approaches.

Checkpoint 2.2

- There are two traditional 'camps' of researcher position in education: positivism and post-positivism.
- Positivists seek objective truths and believe that cause-and-effect relationships exist independently of the researcher or the context in which the research is situated.
- Post-positivists believe that statistical relationships alone are limited; instead, they believe that the context of the research must be taken into account in order to develop meaningful knowledge.
- The most common post-positivist position links to the interpretivist paradigm, which values seeking individuals' perspectives on a given phenomenon (often through talk).
- More researchers in special and inclusive education align themselves with a post-positivist paradigm, but a political focus on academic outcomes means that positivist research is still common.

How to apply your epistemological position to designing a research study

The paradigm that you align yourself with will have a strong impact upon the topic that you choose to research and the methodology that you choose to employ in exploring that topic. As you'll explore in the next chapter, the research questions and aims should always be the main driver of the methodology that you choose. However, your epistemological standpoint will also strongly influence your choice of methodology. For example, if I believe that social interactions support learning, then I am unlikely to conduct a piece of research that doesn't involve some level of discussion/talk. Similarly, If I believe that learning occurs independently of the context in which it is situated, I am unlikely to conduct research that focuses on the social dynamics of the classroom. Many of you reading this book will be practitioners in education, either qualified teachers or those supporting a range of teaching and learning experiences. Therefore, you are likely to be hoping that your educational research informs your professional practice. The case studies below give examples of the ways in which a researcher's epistemological view will impact upon the methodology that they choose to employ in their research. These case studies are focused on empirical research (research that is conducted out in the field in which raw data is gathered from participants) to best support those of you hoping to conduct research in your classrooms/educational contexts.

Case study 2.1

Interpretivist research

Title: 'You have to be like everyone else': Support for students with vision impairment in mainstream secondary schools

Research aims: Opie at al. (2017) were interested in exploring the perspectives of students with vision impairment on the support strategies employed in their schools, to support them with their learning. The study focused on senior secondary students with vision impairment who attended mainstream schools in Victoria, Australia. The researchers composed narrative accounts of the students' experiences, with the overarching aim of determining whether or not the students deemed their school experiences to be inclusive.

Methods: The researchers employed solely qualitative methods; in-depth semi-structured interviews were undertaken with seven participants recruited through the Guide Dog Victoria newsletter. Students who were interested in participating contacted the authors. An interpretive analysis of the students' interviews was undertaken. Once the researchers had drawn out key themes, they met with the participants again to check shared understanding of the data.

Epistemological position: This is an example of an interpretivist study because the researchers were interested in the individualistic perspectives of a small number of participants. The qualitative methodology indicated that the researchers were interested in the stories and narratives that each individual told and were not seeking to make large-scale statistical generalisations about the educational experiences of all students with vision impairment. Although the authors could draw out key themes in terms of the responses of the seven participants, these are 'fuzzy generalisations' (Bassey, 2001)

(Continued)

and are not intended to be generalised to the whole population. Thus, the aim of this research was to draw out themes in relation to inclusive education for a small number of students with vision impairment, which could then be explored further in additional larger-scale research.

Reference: Opie, J., Deppeler, J. and Southcott, J. (2017). 'You have to be like everyone else': Support for students with vision impairment in mainstream secondary schools. *Support for Learning, 32*(3): 267–87.

Case study 2.2

Positivist research

Title: Identifying the impact of developmental coordination disorder (DCD) on educational achievement in secondary school

Research aims: Harrowell et al. (2018) were interested in identifying how a diagnosis of developmental coordination disorder (DCD) impacted upon the GCSE results achieved by these children at age 16 in England. DCD affects both fine and gross motor skills and is known to impact upon school productivity, often due to physical barriers. The researchers wanted to undertake a large-scale study, involving hundreds of participants to make generalisations about the impact of DCD on academic attainment.

Methods: In order to explore the above, the researchers conducted a longitudinal study (one that takes place over a long period of time with set points of data collection throughout). They collected data from two sources: the Avon Longitudinal Study of Parents and Children (ALSPAC) and the GCSE results of a range of children in a given year. The authors analysed the GCSE results from a selection of those diagnosed with DCD, as well as a large control group of children who were not affected by DCD, to make large-scale generalisations about the ways in which DCD affects academic attainment.

Epistemological position: The researchers of this study aligned themselves with a positivist paradigm. This is because they were interested in seeking objective data in order to make large-scale generalisations with the intention of generating universal truths. They were aiming to demonstrate cause-and-effect relationships between the presence of DCD and academic attainment, which were context independent. The researchers in this study were not interested in understanding how DCD may have affected children's experiences of education on an individual level; instead they were solely interested in statistical relationships between two variables on a large scale.

Reference: Harrowell, I., Hollén, L., Lingam, R. and Emond, A. (2018) The impact of developmental coordination disorder on educational achievement in secondary school. *Research in Developmental Disabilities, 72*: 13–22.

Towards a 'third camp' in epistemology

Having read the case studies above and the sections on epistemology in this chapter so far, many of you may be thinking that your views do not neatly fit into one of the 'two camps' of researcher position that we have explored. It is very easy to view positivism as entirely opposite to that of post-positivism or interpretivism. However, there is an emerging school of thinking that there are ways to appreciate the value of the two paradigms by combining some of the approaches advocated by the 'two camps'. This is what could be termed a balanced approach or a 'third camp' in researcher positioning.

As you read more widely, you will find that authors have very different perspectives on the value and place of this third camp; however, in our experience, having worked with students researching in special and inclusive education, this 'third camp' can provide a very useful balance between the two traditional approaches. There are many criticisms of positivism and of post-positivism, so it is helpful to develop a way of thinking that attempts to mitigate some of these criticisms and balance the need for universal laws with the importance of seeking perspectives from individuals.

At a basic level, the third camp in epistemological thinking can be linked to a mixed methods methodological approach. This approach combines the scientific rigour of quantitative methodology with the more subjective, individual-led qualitative approaches. A growing number of the undergraduate and master's-level students that we have supervised elect to undertake a mixed methods approach to their data collection in special and inclusive education. The nature of research involving individuals with special educational needs and/ or disabilities (SEND) means that that there must be some level of appreciation for the individual; it is always difficult to group children homogenously because of their unique nature. However, it is even harder to do this with children with SEND because of the particular barriers to learning they face as individuals. It is therefore difficult to implement a research methodology that follows a solely positivist epistemology in this field. On the other hand, there is a need to undertake research that is relevant to larger groups of individuals with SEND due to the structure of education systems. Research that focuses solely on the opinions of individuals will be limited in its usefulness at policy level. Therefore, the place for research that leans towards a positivist viewpoint (such as that explained in Case study 2.2) is justified.

Tashakkori and Teddlie (2003) note that it is important to make a distinction between mixed methods and mixed models when presenting this alternative epistemological viewpoint. They argue that mixed methods combine quantitative and qualitative methods in the data-collection phase of a study only. However, mixed model studies combine quantitative and qualitative methods throughout all stages of the research process (to include conceptualising a study, planning it, designing the methodology, approaching the data analysis and drawing conclusions). Therefore, it is vital that you explore how far you align yourself with this 'third camp' of researcher position before you plan your study. It may be that you decide to implement methods that are mixed in nature when you collect your data, but this alone may not mean that you buy into a third model of researcher position. Unless you allow the mixed model to permeate all stages of your study, you may find yourself leaning more towards one of the two traditional camps and will need to recognise this in your write-up.

Case study 2.3 highlights a strong example of a mixed methods study in special and inclusive education in order to identify effective ways in which the two traditional researcher camps can be brought together to enable a different approach to conducting research in education.

Case study 2.3

Mixed methods approach

Title: Evaluating the social impacts of inclusion through a multi-method research design

Research aims: The principal aim of Avramidis and Wilde's (2010) study was to investigate the social position of pupils identified with SEND in mainstream settings and their perceived identity. The researchers were particularly interested in identifying what types of social position children with SEND occupy within common social networks and whether or not the children themselves had a sense of what their social position was within the wider groupings.

Methods: The research took place in seven primary schools in one area in the north of England. All pupils enrolled in years 5 and 6 participated in the study resulting in a sample of 566 children. The study adopted a multi-method research design consisting of: sociometric techniques ascertaining the social position of pupils identified with SEND (a quantitative method); a psychometric assessment of pupils' perceptions of themselves resulting in an in-depth exploration of the multidimensional nature of their self-concepts (a second quantitative method); and qualitative interviewing of professionals in the seven participating schools with a view to examining individual teacher and institutional approaches to inclusion.

Epistemological position: This study is an example of what Tashakkori and Teddie (2003) would term a 'mixed model' study, as the authors have clearly implemented a mixed methods epistemological viewpoint throughout all stages of the research. The authors commence the justification of their methodology by highlighting the limited capacity of solely qualitative methodology in capturing impacts of inclusion on the behaviour, social skills, attitudes and friendships of children with and without SEND. They highlight that qualitative studies into the experience of students with SEND have great value in articulating personal perceptions and accounts of school experience, but the authors of this study aimed to go a step further by aiming to make generalisations that pertain to large groups of children. The authors state that their 'synthesis of sociometric and psychometric techniques achieved our objective of finding a more balanced quantitative approach which could shed more light on both the social and affective outcomes of inclusion' (p.330).

Reference: Avramidis, E. and Wilde, A. (2009) Evaluating the social impacts of inclusion through a multi-method research design. *Education 3–13*, 37(4): 323–34.

Chapter summary

This chapter has introduced you to the complex world of the 'ologies', with a specific focus on common epistemological viewpoints in special and inclusive education. As you will now be aware, there is a vast array of complex terminology to familiarise yourself with, in order to identify your personal researcher position. However, this complex terminology can be simplified by highlighting the core differences between the positivist and post-positivist paradigms. It is likely that, as a result of the case studies and activity in this chapter, you will find more affinity with one of these two camps of researcher position. Indeed, you may feel that the more novel third camp aligns most effectively with your epistemological viewpoint. Whichever camp you feel best reflects your researcher position, you will be able to take this forward to support you in navigating the remainder of this book. We will now move on to exploring the ways in which you plan a study in special and inclusive education effectively, and your researcher position will be integral to the decisions that you make as your research unfolds.

Recommended reading

- Chapters 1 and 2 in Cohen, L., Manion, L. and Morrison, K. (2018) *Research Methods in Education*. London: Routledge.

Outline: This is a very useful introductory text for those of you who are unfamiliar with the 'ologies'. It includes an in-depth discussion of the different assumptions that underpin positivist and interpretivist approaches to research and how they influence different ideas about 'truth' and social reality. It also provides some useful endorsements and counterarguments in relation to the value of a range of epistemological viewpoints and accompanying paradigms, common to educational research.

- Chapter 1 in Creswell, J.W. and Creswell, J.D. (2018) *Research Design: Qualitative, Quantitative and Mixed Methods Approaches*. London: Sage.

Outline: This text was one of the first to compare the merits of qualitative, quantitative and mixed methods approaches and the arguments within it are often pertinent to research in educational contexts. This chapter explores epistemology as an important precursor to the selection of a research approach.

- Chapter 1 in Kumar, R. (2019) *Research Methodology: A Step-by-Step Guide for Beginners*. London: Sage.

Outline: This text is written in an accessible format; the author has taken care to provide in-text definitions of complex terminology as it is being introduced, often in the page margins. The important concepts are presented in coloured text, which also helps with navigation. This text is not written for a specific audience of educational researchers, but Chapter 1 does give some useful food for thought in articulating a 'way of thinking' when approaching research in the social sciences.

- Scotland, J. (2012) Exploring the philosophical underpinnings of research: Relating ontology and epistemology to the methodology and methods of the scientific, interpretive, and critical research paradigms. *English Language Teaching*, 5(9): 9–16.

Outline: This paper provides a comprehensive outline of the emergence of various ontological and epistemological viewpoints in educational research. It explores the philosophical underpinnings of three major educational research paradigms: scientific, interpretive and critical. The paper is particularly useful in helping you to explore the interrelationships between each paradigm's ontology, epistemology, methodology and methods. It is very well written and available publicly via Google Scholar.

Activity 2.1 answers

1. positivist 2. positivist 3. post-positivist 4. post-positivist 5. post-positivist 6. positivist 7. positivist 8. positivist 9. post-positivist

3

GETTING STARTED: DEVELOPING A RESEARCH STUDY IN SPECIAL AND INCLUSIVE EDUCATION

━━━━━━━━━━ Chapter objectives ━━━━━━━━━━

By the end of this chapter you will:

- ✓ Have some ideas about how to generate possible research topics
- ✓ Understand the purpose of research questions
- ✓ Know what differentiates a good research question from a poor research question
- ✓ Recognise the difference between aims and objectives
- ✓ Appreciate the wide range of factors that need to be considered when planning your research

'You don't have to be great to start, but you have to start to be great.'

Introduction

The quote above by American motivational speaker Zig Ziglar offers a useful reminder that research is a process. Although it might seem daunting at the beginning, taking those first few steps often results in students becoming more confident and willing to take ownership and control of their research. This chapter aims to support you in this process.

There are arguably three main questions that need to be considered at the start of a project: What to study? Why study it? How to study it? In answering these questions you will need to make decisions about:

- *Your general research topic*: Broad area of interest
- *Your research question*: The specific focus or aim of the study
- *Your research design*: The general strategy that guides the research
- *Your research methods*: The specific strategies and techniques used for collecting and analysing data

This chapter deals with the first two decision points. We begin with some of the strategies that our students have found helpful for identifying and choosing their research topics. We then move to how a broad topic can be distilled into a specific research question. We also identify potential challenges and the need for early consideration of research participants and settings.

Research topic: Deciding what to research

The task of identifying your general research topic and then narrowing that down to a specific and feasible project is not always easy. You might be keen to move quickly into the data-collection phase of your project but taking the time to work carefully through the initial planning stage will save you time and anxious moments later in the research process.

Key question 1: Is the research about something that really interests you?

It is important that you choose a topic about which you are genuinely interested. Undertaking research is a time-consuming and demanding process so a genuine inter-est in your topic will help keep you motivated over the course of your project. You can be sure that things will not always go according to plan and there will inevitably be aspects of a project that you find less interesting than others. This will vary from project to project, and from researcher to researcher. Some researchers enjoy transcribing their recorded interviews as this gives them a slow-motion review of what was said. Others find this process laborious. Some find reviewing the literature an exciting process as they discover new things about their chosen topic – others less so, particularly if locating information relevant to their chosen topic is proving to be challenging. Sometimes it is difficult to access appropriate participants for research, or arrangements are changed at the last minute and need to be re-scheduled. These are just three examples of the many factors that will impact on your research journey. They are offered to make the point that there will inevitably be challenges along the way and that many aspects of a project take longer, or require a higher degree of perseverance, than initially anticipated. This is why it is important to choose a topic that you are genuinely interested in.

Burton et al. (2014) suggest that your research should, in addition to being of genuine interest, 'offer the possibility of meaningful gains' (Burton et al., 2014: 25). We agree. For students reading this book, undertaking a research project may be a requirement of your course. Gaining the award for which you are working is obviously an important benefit. But look beyond that. How might your research also contribute to your personal or professional growth? If you are a practitioner researcher, can your chosen topic connect with a specific concern or priority in your setting? If you are a student researcher, is learning more about your chosen topic likely to be of benefit in your future work. Perhaps your chosen topic connects with a specific policy or to national concerns? Whatever the case, a meaningful connection with your current or future professional practice will also help to maintain motivation over the course of your research.

Checkpoint 3.1

Choose a topic about which you are genuinely interested and which might also be of benefit to your current or future professional work.

Research topic: Some pointers

If you don't already have a burning interest you would like to pursue through research, use the following prompts to help stimulate your thinking.

1   What have you been reading or learning about in other parts of your programme of study that you would like to know more about?

Example: Sophie developed an interest in Makaton after completing the level 2 Makaton training that was offered as an optional part of her degree in special and inclusive education. Over her summer break she accessed additional literature about Makaton and visited a nursery that had begun using it as part of their everyday practices. These experiences influenced her desire to learn more about Makaton and how it might support inclusive practices. Her final-year research project provided a good opportunity to do so.

2   Has an experience in your work or placement settings sparked an interest in a
     topic?

Example: Moana was a practising teacher who was concurrently working towards her
master's degree in Education. She had become interested in fetal alcohol spectrum disorder (FASD) as a result of having a child with FASD in her class. She had found herself
ill-prepared to work effectively with this child and began reading around the topic and
talking with colleagues. She learned that her colleagues felt similarly ill-equipped to
work effectively with FASD and other conditions that affect learning and behaviour.
Moana wondered how widespread her experiences were and what sorts of strategies
and resources would be helpful in supporting such children. These experiences and
thoughts provided a useful starting point when it was time for her to begin her master's
thesis.

3   Is there a topic relevant to special and inclusive education that has been
     highlighted in the media lately?

'Thousands of children with special needs excluded from school' (The *Guardian*, 23
October 2018, https://tinyurl.com/ybasvhl5)
     Example: Scott, a teacher trainee, became interested in the relationship between school
exclusions and pupils with SEND after coming across the headline above. He researched
the Department for Education statistics (see DfE, 2019) to find that pupils with SEND
were indeed disproportionately represented in the exclusion statistics. He also looked
for other similar headlines and found that this issue was not confined just to the UK but
was also present in other English-speaking countries. He talked with his classmates about
why this might be and found himself wanting to know more. He decided that something
related to this general topic would provide an interesting and relevant focus for his final-
year research project.

4   Have there been any recent policy changes that might have a particular impact on
     learners with SEND?

Example: Talia worked for a local authority in England and part of her professional role
required her to work closely with special educational needs coordinators (SENCOs).
She began her doctoral studies shortly after the introduction of the revised *Special
Educational Needs and Disability Code of Practice* (DfE and DH, 2015). The changes that
the new *Code of Practice* heralded for both SENCOs and pupils with SEND provided
many possibilities for research topics that would also connect with Talia's day-to-day
work.
     The prompts above are just a few ways that might help you get started. Journal articles
offer another fruitful avenue as they report the latest research and often focus on topical
issues. Television documentaries, TED talks and social media posts have provided other
sources of inspiration for our students.

Opening up possibilities: Brainstorming strategies

Once you have identified a general topic you need to narrow it down to something more focused and manageable. Mind maps or spider diagrams can be a useful way of beginning this process as they provide a visual representation of all your thoughts about a topic in a relational way. There are different ways of constructing such diagrams but they typically involve starting with your main idea in the middle and your related thoughts branching out from it. These might include ways in which your main topic connects to the wider educational context, what different stakeholders think, and what theories, policies and practices are relevant to your chosen topic. You may want to reorganise your initial structure as you start to see which items relate more closely to others or can be logically grouped together. Several iterations of your mind map may therefore be needed before you are satisfied that it captures most of the relevant information upon which to base your research decisions.

Remember that mind maps and spider diagrams can include pictures, charts, icons and symbols as well as words. You can use colour, shape and outlining as ways of structuring your thoughts and representing links between different parts. There are also apps that can support you to create and manipulate an electronic version of a mindmap (www. miro.com, www.mindmeister.com and www.coggle.it are just three examples). The main thing is to be flexible and create your mindmap in a way that works best for you. You will find that the process as well as the final product is a great way of stimulating thoughts, generating new ideas and helping you to see the connections between different aspects of your topic.

Some students find it useful to accompany their mind map with a three-column chart that lists: (1) things I already know about my topic; (2) things I think I know but am not sure about; (3) things I don't know but would like to know. If you think you already know something, be sure to reflect on your evidence base. In other words, identify how it is that you know something. Sometimes this process results in students questioning some of their prior assumptions about a topic. Identifying and questioning assumptions (your own, those of others and those implied within policy) is an important element of approaching your topic with a critical but open mind. The *Guardian* headline presented earlier caught Scott's eye because he thought that fewer pupils with SEND would be excluded from school. This was based on his assumption that once a school had identified a child as having SEND, they would put the necessary supports in place. It was only once he checked the DfE statistics that he learned that pupils with SEND were indeed disproportionately represented in the exclusion statistics. This made him want to understand why this might be.

Finally, share your mind map and chart so that others can see what you've been thinking. Discussing your ideas with classmates, friends, course lecturers and other professionals will help consolidate and refine your thoughts and also help you to identify any personal biases or misconceptions that you hold. These early activities are likely to generate new ideas and interests relevant to your broad topic. You are also likely to start seeing the connections between different ideas and the multitude of possibilities in terms of what direction your research could take. This is good. You may find that your interests shift and change so it is important to be open to new possibilities and to allow plenty of time for this initial stage of the research process.

Checkpoint 3.2

Allow plenty of time for the brainstorming and planning stage of your project.

So far, we have suggested some ways in which you might go about identifying an appropriate topic. We have emphasised the importance of choosing a research topic that is of genuine interest to you and of allowing enough time to identify and consider multiple research possibilities. Once you have decided on your research topic, it is time to specify the exact focus of your study. This is where research questions come in.

Research questions

Almost all research texts stress the importance of the research question. In the following section we explain why the research question is considered so important and highlight some of the elements that differentiate a good research question from a poor one. We also explain the difference between aims and objectives and their relationship to the research question.

The value of research questions

A good research question transforms a general topic or area of interest into a focused and feasible investigation. Its key purpose is to clarify the specific aims and limits of a study. This helps to keep the researcher focused during the research and also to communicate the key aim of the research to others. A research question, with its accompanying objectives, also provides an indication of how you plan to answer it. In other words, it will guide decisions about the study design, the sorts of data that need to be collected, how and from whom. As Roberts (2018) points out, when you are clear about the question, some research designs and methods will be ruled out while others will be more suitable.

Constructing a research question may take some time and require several iterations. A common challenge is finding the right balance between breadth and specificity. A good research question needs to be broad enough to connect with the wider educational context. This ensures that it will be of interest and have relevance to others. But it also needs to be focused enough so that its specific purpose is clear and answerable within the available time and resources.

Activity 3.1

Research questions

Read the three questions below and identify which is too broad, which is too narrow and which is about right. Review your decisions and then modify the 'too broad' and 'too narrow' questions to make them better. You can find our thoughts about these questions at the end of the chapter.

1   How do resources in a special school impact children with SEND?
2   Does the Nessy Learning Programme support the literacy development of Lana, a primary school pupil whose first language is not English?
3   What factors influence the college choices of students with MLD in relation to whether they continue studying physical education at post-16 level?

Aims and objectives

Research questions are often discussed in relation to research aims and objectives. Thomson (2020) refers to research aims as the 'what' of research (what you are trying to understand, learn more about or achieve with your research), while objectives are the 'how' (what you actually need to do to achieve your aim). She explains that an aim is therefore generally expressed in broad terms and in the form 'to + action' (for example, to explore, investigate, evaluate or describe). In journal articles, you'll sometimes see the word 'purpose' used instead of aim. Either way, you'll notice that the aim or purpose of the research is expressed in broad terms. It will align closely with the research question and there will generally be only one or two.

Objectives, on the other hand, indicate the specific steps that need to be taken to achieve the stated aim. In other words, they break the main aim or research question into a number of smaller, manageable pieces. While a research project will normally have only one key aim and research question, it will have several objectives. Many of our students find that between three and six objectives is an appropriate number for a research dissertation or master's thesis. Constructing and reviewing research aims and objectives will help you to be clear about what it is you want to achieve and how you will go about achieving it. It is important to check that each objective makes a specific contribution to the overall aim of the project.

Activity 3.2

Research aims and questions

Below you will find the title and first part of an abstract from a journal article. Read them to identify the research aim. Summarise the aim in your own words and then formulate a research question for the stated aim.

(Continued)

Title: Perceptions of inclusive education: a mixed methods investigation of parental attitudes in three Australian primary schools

Abstract: Growing numbers of families now enrol their children in inclusive schools. The purpose of this research was to investigate the perceptions of 44 Australian parents. Eight parents had children with disabilities and 36 had children who are typically developing. Data were collected using a questionnaire incorporating the Attitudes Towards Inclusion/ Mainstreaming scale and a focus group for parents of children with disabilities. Parents all agreed that inclusive education benefits their children. Satisfaction with inclusion scores was similar and although parents of typically developing children expressed greater satisfaction, the difference was not significant. Parents of children with disabilities were significantly more likely to strongly agree that children have the right to inclusive education. Most parents felt that teachers are not well prepared to support the diverse range of students with disabilities in inclusive classrooms.

Reference: Stevens, L. and Wurf, G. (2020) Perceptions of inclusive education: A mixed-methods investigation of parental attitudes in three Australian primary schools. *International Journal of Inclusive Education*, 24(4): 351–65.

The title and abstract indicate that the aim of the research could be summarised along the following lines: *This research aimed to explore parental perceptions of inclusive education.* You might have used some different words such as *investigate* instead of *explore* or *attitudes towards* instead of *perceptions of*, but the meaning should have been along similar lines. This example illustrates how an aim is expressed in broad and general terms and there is usually just one. The research question, on the other hand, is more specific. For the above project it might have read something along the lines of: *What attitudes do the parents of children in three Australian primary schools have towards inclusive education?* You can see that the research question reveals additional information about the limits of the research, such as where it took place and what phase of education it relates to.

If you were to read the full article, you would see that the researchers also state three research objectives. These are to find out whether:

- parents hold favourable perceptions towards inclusion and their satisfaction with their child's progress in inclusive classes
- parents of typically developing children hold more favourable attitudes towards inclusion than parents of children with disabilities
- parents of children with disabilities are concerned with current levels of support and training within schools to effectively implement inclusive practices (p.355).

You can see how each objective makes a specific contribution to the more general aim of investigating parental perceptions about inclusive education. You can also see that exploring whether these differ between parents of typically developing children and parents of children with disabilities was a distinct element of the research.

Case study 3.1

Over the course of her studies in special and inclusive education, Taya had become increasingly interested in how ASD affects children's learning, sociability and behaviour. Her interest was reinforced through part-time work as a teaching assistant in a mainstream school where she had an opportunity to support several children who had been diagnosed as having ASD. As a future educational practitioner, Taya was keen to learn more about how schools could ensure the successful inclusion of learners with ASD. This meant that Taya was highly motivated to pursue a research study in this area. She would clearly benefit from completing her degree but there was also potential benefit for her future work and for the children she currently worked with in her role as a teaching assistant.

Taya's broad area of interest (her research topic) was therefore about what can be done to support the educational inclusion of learners with ASD. Taya's next task was to transform this broad research topic into a more specific research question with an accompanying set of objectives. Her initial research question was:

How can schools promote the inclusion of pupils with ASD?

This question was too broad and all-encompassing, and given the vast amount of research that has already been undertaken about ASD it was also hard to judge what it might contribute to what is already known. Taya worked on her question further and came up with:

What strategies and resources can support the inclusion of pupils with ASD?

This is a little more focused but still too broad. The research question needs to indicate the boundaries of the research. Which pupils, which setting, which phase of education, what specific focus? Taya's next iteration narrowed her focus further.

What strategies and resources can support the communication skills of Key Stage 1 children (5–7-year-olds) with ASD who attend a mainstream school?

She then used this to formulate the following objectives.

- To review the range of strategies and resources that are thought to support the communication skills of children with ASD
- To gather staff perceptions of the strategies used to support the communication skills of three case study children in one mainstream primary school
- To observe how these children respond to strategies aimed at supporting their communication skills

---

This example illustrates how Taya had to re-work her research question several times. The process prompted her to think through carefully a number of possible research directions until she identified the specific focus she wanted to take. In the remainder of the chapter we focus in greater depth on how the 'worthiness' of a project might be evaluated and some of the practical matters that need to be considered in relation to the feasibility of your project.

Key question 2: Is the research worthwhile?

A second question to consider when deciding what to research is the extent to which it would be considered worthwhile. In other words, will it be of interest to others and will it build on what is already known about a topic? To answer this question, think about *why* you want to answer your particular research question. Why is it important, what will it contribute to new knowledge or understanding, and who else will be interested in what you find out? Is there already a lot of information available that relates to your research question? If so, will you be able to add something new? Reading widely will help you establish the extent to which this is the case. It will also ensure that you become familiar with current policy, terminology and different stakeholder perceptions relevant to your chosen question. We develop this further in Chapter 5, which focuses on the place of the literature review in research, but for present purposes the important point is that establishing the extent to which your research question is worthwhile requires reasonable familiarity with issues, policies and perceptions relevant to your research question. The better informed you are at the beginning of your project, the better it is likely to be (Mutch, 2013). This is why some prior reading is important before you formulate your research question.

Another criterion that is often used to judge the merits of a research project is that of originality. For university-based research, there is an expectation that postgraduate projects make an original contribution to the collective knowledge base. This is less the case for undergraduate projects but is still a useful criterion to bear in mind. At this point you might well be thinking that education has been such a well-researched area, how can I possibly contribute something new or original? Surely it's all been done before?

This is not necessarily the case. Lambert suggests three ways that you might achieve an element of originality. The first relates to the research setting. He points out that it is 'likely that no one has researched this topic in the particular education setting where you will investigate it' (2012: 60). Many readers of this book will be undertaking small-scale research that is specific to one or a small number of settings. While this means that key findings are inevitably non-generalisable and may have limited application to other (different) settings, it also means that the research outcomes will be new and have particular relevance to those settings. This makes the research worthwhile and original.

Lambert's second point relates to methodology and the possibility that your research will be innovative in its design or data-collection methods. This book will help. In Chapter 1 we highlighted the marginalisation of pupil voice in much educational research and in Chapter 9 we present some innovative ways of enabling children and young people's understandings and experiences to be brought to the fore. We encourage researchers to use innovative methods alongside more traditional research methods as a way of shedding new light on current understandings about the educational experiences of learners with SEND.

Lambert's third point is that you may reach different conclusions from other research. This is quite likely for small-scale research that is tied to a specific setting. Finally, as

Roberts (2018) points out, no theory or understanding or methodology is ever truly original because all of our ideas (whether or not we are aware of this) are informed by those that came before us. Originality therefore 'emerges in the way we interpret, synthesise, compare, contest, and apply ideas' (Lambert, 2012: 31). This is another reason why reading widely will support good research outcomes.

Checkpoint 3.3

Familiarise yourself with literature, theory and policy relevant to your research topic before finalising your research question.

Key question 3: Is the research feasible?

A research question clearly needs to be answerable, but it also needs to be answerable within particular parameters. If your project is for a university degree, certain aspects will be prescribed. For example, you will be required to adhere to a specific word limit and will be given a deadline by which to complete your project. These constraints mean that you need to plan carefully and to consider the wide range of factors that might help or hinder the successful and timely completion of your project. The examples below illustrate three commonly occurring factors that students should consider when evaluating the feasibility of their research.

Time

Some data-collection methods are more time consuming than others. If, for example, you intend to use interviews as a data-collection method and also plan to audio-record and transcribe them, you need to factor in the time this will take. We encourage our students to do a pilot interview and transcribe it. This not only allows them to practise their interviewing technique but also helps them to realise how long the transcription process takes. Many research texts suggest a transcription time of four times the interview time. So, for a one-hour interview, you need to allow four hours for transcription. Some students amend the number of interviews they plan to undertake as a result of this pilot interview and transcribing process.

If you are researching with children, for example doing some interviews or a walking tour or engaging them in an activity, you need to consider their developmental needs and capabilities. If concentration spans are likely to be short, how might you build in breaks? Might you need to conduct your interview or activity over several sessions?

If your research is with a child with ASD who may become anxious when encountering new people and situations, how do you plan to prepare them adequately to engage with the research tasks and with you as a researcher? If pre-research visits would help, the time required needs to be factored into your planning.

Knowledge and skills

Particularly if you are new to research, you need to consider the extent to which you have the necessary knowledge and expertise to carry out your project. This might include the ability to use equipment, deploy an intervention, take a particular sort of measure or communicate with certain participants. If you don't have enough hands-on experience to use your planned methods competently, consider how you can you get some extra practice. Our students have found that the time it takes to pilot (test out) an aspect of their research almost always paid off later with better quality data than they would otherwise have gathered. Gaining additional experience might involve: practising your interview technique with classmates or colleagues; checking out how children respond to a particular activity by trying it out with nephews and nieces or other children in the setting; familiarising yourself with some educational software by using it yourself; or practising a specific data-gathering technique with other children.

Example: Andy's research required him to take 'running records' and do a miscue analysis of the literacy skills of a group of children (see Clay, 2019, for more on these techniques). He understood the theory and knew what he needed to do but when he tested his skills on a young relative, he found that putting this knowledge into practice was harder than he thought. He practised his technique on several other children until he felt confident enough to apply his skills to the research.

Physical resources and consumables

Ensuring that your research question is feasible also requires you to identify any equipment or physical resources that are needed. These might include recording devices, educational software, materials for activities with children, or equipment, such as cameras or tablets, that you might want children to use as part of your research. Do you have what you need? If not, can you borrow them? Many universities have technical equipment that students can borrow, but bear in mind that often they must be booked in advance or are only lent out for very short periods. You also need to assess the cost of any consumables such as stationery, photocopying or physical resources. Travel to and from settings is another expense that needs to be considered when thinking through the feasibility of your study.

Key question 4: Where will your research take place, and who will enable it?

Once you have established your research topic and question, you next need to consider the different ways you might go about answering your research question. Many projects will involve primary research and thus some fieldwork. This means that you need to make decisions about where your research will take place (research setting) and who will be involved (research participants).

Many of the projects undertaken by our students have occurred in an early years or school context, either mainstream or special settings, or sometimes both. But this is not exclusively the case. Our students have also undertaken their projects in Sure Start centres, alternative education centres, children's homes, children's hospital wards or supported housing facilities for young people with learning disabilities. Others have worked with charities that deliver specific services such as animal, music or play therapy or offer various after-school clubs.

For some students, gaining access to an appropriate setting or participants can be a challenging and time-consuming process. There are two main reasons for this. First, there will almost always be gatekeepers (people whose permission you need in order to undertake research in a particular setting). Concerns about safeguarding vulnerable children and young adults can make gaining access difficult. Additionally, there will often be several levels of gatekeepers whose permission you need in order to proceed with your research. For research in English schools, for example, you would need to start by seeking the agreement of the headteacher and governing body or trust board.

Second, settings such as schools, nurseries and Sure Start centres are busy places in which staff are often faced with multiple competing demands. A cold call from an unknown student wanting to undertake research in their setting is unlikely to be afforded a high priority. Additionally, gatekeepers may have some statutory duties with which they must comply. Where children (or adults considered to be vulnerable) are involved, many organisations are legally required to undertake checks before allowing someone to work or undertake research in a setting. These checks can have cost implications for the setting and may therefore be a barrier.

One way of mitigating some of these barriers is to use contacts that you already have when looking for a setting within which to undertake your research. Many of our students undertake placements as part of their studies. These experiences frequently result in a student developing an interest in a particular topic and additionally a relationship of trust within that setting. As Abbott and Langston point out, 'those in which relationships are well established and links have already been made are often welcoming and amenable to research being undertaken' (2005: 43). Burton et al. (2014) add that a researcher will be much more likely to be supported in their research if there are some clear connections between what you'd like to research and one or more priorities for the organisation. In other words, think about how the setting and participants might benefit from the research.

Checkpoint 3.4

Evaluate all of the factors that might impact on the feasibility of your study.

Chapter summary

This chapter has emphasised the importance of careful planning when you begin your research project in special and inclusive education. It has offered some practical strategies for identifying your research topic and some exemplars of how this might be narrowed down to a focused and viable research question. We have structured the chapter around four key questions. You should be able to answer 'yes' to each of these before proceeding with your project.

1   Is the research about something that really interests you?
2   Is the research worthwhile?
3   Is the research feasible?
4   Have you identified where your research will take place and who will enable it?

We have intentionally avoided an additional important question. Is your research ethical? We consider ethics to be so integral to the whole research process that we dedicate a discrete chapter to this topic. We move to this important aspect of research in the next chapter.

Recommended reading

- Chapter 1 in Thomas, G. (2017) *How to Do Your Research Project: A Guide for Students.* London: Sage.

Outline: Although not written specifically for educational researchers, many of the examples used in this text are education related. This introductory chapter provides a brief overview of different purposes of research, different types of research questions and the sort of evidence that might be sought to answer particular questions.

- Chapter 2 in Lambert, M. (2012) *A Beginner's Guide to Doing Your Education Research Project.* London: Sage.

Outline: This chapter provides a brief but useful overview of the research process as a whole. Structured around the three main phases of planning, doing and analysing research, it identifies the many sub-components that you need to think about *prior to* starting your project.

Research question activity: Our thoughts

Question 1 is too broad. Special schools use a wide range of resources and cater for children with a wide range of SEND. This question could be improved by specifying a narrower focus – for example by focusing on a subset of resources or children with a specific SEND.

Question 2 is very specific. It could work well as a case study and could be useful for a practitioner who wants to support Lana's learning. However, the very narrow focus might mean that the outcomes of the research may be of limited interest to the wider educational community. This does not mean that it is not worthwhile – rather, that it has limited wider applicability.

Question 3 achieves a good balance – it has a specific focus while also being potentially of interest to the wider educational community.

4
ETHICAL CONSIDERATIONS WHEN RESEARCHING SPECIAL AND INCLUSIVE EDUCATION

━━━━━━━━━━ Chapter objectives ━━━━━━━━━━

By the end of this chapter you will:

✓ Understand what is meant by ethical research
✓ Know the key purposes and principles common to ethical codes of practice and why they came about
✓ Have examined potential challenges to ethical research in the field of special and inclusive education and reflect on how they might be addressed
✓ Be able to identify ethical considerations that may not feature explicitly in institutional frameworks and reflect on how they might be addressed

'No discourse, no theory can resolve the unpredictable complexity of ethical dilemmas in research in human sciences' (Mortari and Harcourt, 2012: 239)

Introduction

In Chapter 1 we noted that ethical considerations are intrinsic to all parts of the research process – the gathering of data, how data is analysed, and how research is written up and shared with others (Alderson and Morrow, 2020). We also highlighted that research involving children and young people with SEND brings with it some potential complications that are less typically experienced in research with adults or those without SEND. This point is particularly salient when it comes to research ethics. As a number of scholars have noted, institutional guidance and codes of practice are typically quite general in nature and thus provide little guidance that relates specifically to research with children and young people with SEND (Mortari and Harcourt, 2012; Wall, 2017). Indeed, it is interesting to note that it is only the latest edition of the British Educational Research Association (BERA) (2018) ethical guidelines that draws specific attention to the need for special consideration when working with children. In this chapter we look briefly at the historical context of ethical research practices and identify key principles and concepts considered important for ethical research. We then focus in particular on how these might be applied and what additional issues need to be considered when researching with children or those with SEND.

Historical context, key principles and terms

Ethics, as a discipline, has a long history reaching back at least as far as the early Greek philosophers. Indeed, the word 'ethics' derives from the Greek word *ethos*, meaning character or disposition. In very general terms, ethics is about what is considered 'right' or 'good'. As implied in our lead-in quote, determining what is 'right' or 'good' is often not a straightforward matter.

Contemporary practices relating to research ethics evolved in response to international condemnation of medical research atrocities that took place in the twentieth century, most notoriously those conducted by the Nazis during World War II. It is therefore not surprising that the first formal ethical codes of practice were developed within the biomedical community. An early example is the World Medical Association (1954) *Principles for Those in Research and Experimentation* which stated that participants in medical research should be fully informed about the purpose, methods and possible risks associated with the research and that consent should be obtained in writing beforehand. The principles enshrined in these early medical codes of practice were subsequently adapted and applied within the social sciences.

Around the world, many research organisations have formulated their own ethical codes of practice to which their members are expected to abide. This means that right from the planning stage, researchers need to identify potential ethical issues and consider how they will be addressed. In the UK, most educational researchers are guided by those produced by BERA (2018). Universities also develop their own guidance and have ethics review committees from which both staff and students are required to obtain approval prior to engaging in research. Although codes differ from one another in their length, detail and structure, they are invariably underpinned by the same general principles. These include:

- to treat research participants with dignity and respect
- to cause no harm (sometimes referred to as non-maleficence)
- to maximise benefit (sometimes referred to as beneficence)

Activity 4.1

Before reading on, reflect on what these three general principles might mean in practical terms. In what ways might you treat participants with dignity and respect, avoid harm and ensure some benefit?

These three general principles are operationalised through concepts such as informed consent, the right to withdraw and the protection of privacy. We review what is meant by these terms before looking in more detail at some of the specific issues that might arise when undertaking research with learners with SEND.

Obtaining **consent** refers to the process of seeking participants' agreement to be involved in research. The BERA (2018) guidelines state that consent should be **voluntary**; in other words, potential participants should not feel pressured to give their consent. Consent should also be **informed**. This means that before agreeing to be part of a study, participants understand what the research is about, why it is being undertaken, what is expected of them, and if they take part, what will happen to any data that is collected. Being fully informed implies transparency – in other words, an open and honest process that avoids deception. Additionally, ethical research requires that consent is viewed as an ongoing process. This means that participants should understand their **right to withdraw** from the study at any time, without consequence and without having to explain why.

The **protection of privacy** is another key principle. It refers to ensuring that the identity of those involved in the research, whether it be an institution, group of people or an individual, is not revealed through the research process or outputs. This is often achieved by offering anonymity or confidentiality. **Anonymity** is when no-one (not even the researcher) knows the identity of participants. An online survey that does not record people's real names or the names of educational institutions is an example of a research method that offers anonymity. In research where there is more direct contact between the researcher and participants, for example, in face-to-face interviews or classroom observations, anonymity is not possible. Instead, researchers offer **confidentiality**. In these situations, the researcher knows the identity of participants but takes steps to ensure that it is not evident to others. Ascribing fictional names to individuals or institutions (sometimes referred to as pseudonyms) is a common way of achieving this. Another is modifying or concealing details that might make participants or a setting with particular characteristics potentially identifiable in research outputs.

The **secure storage of data** is another important element in protecting people's privacy. This requires researchers to ensure that electronic data such as research notes, audio recordings or transcriptions are kept on a password-protected computer, and that any physical artefacts such as completed questionnaires, signed consent forms, paper copies of transcripts, observations, field notes or children's drawings are kept in a secure location such as a locked filing cabinet. The BERA (2018) guidelines note that if any data are going to be shared with others, this needs to be made explicit right at the start. Your research supervisor, for example, might view some of your raw data – so this needs to be clear in the information that is provided to prospective participants.

Similarly, potential participants need to be informed about any **benefits** or **harms** that might result from taking part in research. You might be thinking, 'What possible harm? Of course I'm not going to harm anyone!' The medical research atrocities of the past, where people were physically harmed and forced to undergo painful or life-limiting procedures, are clear examples of harm that would never be approved by ethics committees today. Neither would the severe emotional distress caused to participants in past psychological experiments such as those conducted by Stanley Milgram in the 1960s. His infamous research of people's compliance with authority figures was heavily criticised for the deception involved and the resulting distress caused to participants (see Recommended reading at the end of the chapter if you want to learn more about this).

Practices that seek voluntary informed consent, avoid deception and protect people's privacy go a long way to avoiding harm in social science research generally – but what possible harms or 'costs' to participants might there be in educational research?

The BERA (2018) guidance draws attention to the time, effort or inconvenience of participating in educational research as a cost to participants. Additionally, research fatigue might be experienced by schools or groups of people who are frequently approached to be part of someone's research project. Many of our students are reminded of this first hand when their invitations to schools to be involved in research either go unanswered or the response is 'no'. A student clearly benefits from the research if it helps them complete a qualification for which they are studying, but what are the costs to those who enable that research and how do they benefit in return? Does removing pupils from their classrooms for research purposes constitute harm? What are they missing out on while they are with you? Might your presence in a classroom for observational purposes be a disruptive distraction for some learners? Could discussing certain topics or experiences cause discomfort or subsequent emotional distress? While you can never be 100 per cent sure that your research will cause no harm, taking the time to consider the possible costs and benefits for participants beforehand, and to point these out to participants, is an important part of ethical practice.

Application of key principles

In much social science research, informed consent is typically sought by providing prospective participants with a written information sheet that explains key details about the research. An information sheet should explain: the purpose of the research; what participation would involve (for example, completing an online survey, being interviewed or observed, being part of a focus group or an intervention); where, how and when the research would take place; and how much time that would take. It should also explain what data will be collected and how; what will happen to any data that is collected; how privacy will be protected; and whether there are any possible risks or benefits that might result from being part of the study. There should also be a clear statement that participation is voluntary and that participants can withdraw from the study at any point without having to explain why. For students, university ethics committees normally require you to include the name and contact details of your supervisor and who to contact in the case of a complaint. There is also an expectation that both staff and student researchers gain written confirmation that participants understand the research and agree to participate. This is usually achieved through a separate consent form to which participants add their name, signature and date and which is retained by the researcher. In situations where this is not possible because there is no physical contact with participants, such as in an internet-based survey, confirmation of voluntary informed consent is typically gained through including a statement such as, 'By (completing this questionnaire), you are indicating that you understand the research and voluntarily agree to participate.'

Researching with children and young people with SEND

If your study, or a part of your study, involves the direct participation of children and young people with SEND, there may be some specific issues that require additional consideration when putting ethical principles into practice. Before reading on, reflect on what some of these might be. Then complete the activity below.

Activity 4.2

Ethical tensions and issues

The link below takes you to a five-minute video clip in which Associate Professor Nicola Taylor* shares her thoughts on ethical research involving children.

https://tinyurl.com/yaq5sz45

(Continued)

As you watch this clip:

1   Identify one of the key tensions that may arise when undertaking research with children. (Clue: this relates to competing rights, which Nicola describes as requiring a 'delicate balance'.)
2   Identify some of the specific ethical dilemmas that may arise when undertaking research with children and listen out for Nicola's ideas on how they might be resolved.
3   The clip focuses on children. What other groups of learners might similar concerns apply to?

*Associate Professor Taylor is the director of the Children's Issues Centre, University of Otago, New Zealand. She was part of an international team that developed UNICEF's Ethical Research Involving Children compendium (see Recommended reading at the end of this chapter).

Possible issues when researching with children

In the video clip activity, Nicola makes the point that there is a tension between a child's right to be heard in matters that affect them and a child's right to protection. She identifies three specific issues that need to be considered when researching with children. The first is the possibility that speaking about sensitive issues might cause distress. Ethical research requires the researcher to consider whether it is appropriate to ask about certain things, and to review how particular topics might be broached in a sensitive way that minimise the possibility of causing distress. Second, there is the possibility that a child discloses information that adults in their life would be unhappy about. This issue is resolved through mechanisms that protect privacy, such as ensuring anonymity in research outputs. The third issue is one of child protection. If a child discloses information that indicates they are at risk of harm then the researcher has an ethical responsibility to ensure that the child gets access to appropriate support services. This means that assurances of confidentiality in research always have limits and it is important that these are communicated clearly to participants as part of the consent-seeking process. Finally, Nicola speaks about an issue we raised in Chapter 1 – the difference between research *on* and research *with* children – and that the latter has implications for ethical research. She raises these points in relation to children but they are equally applicable to young people and adults with SEND. We examine some of these in greater depth below.

Rethinking informed consent

When researching with young children, those with learning or sensory disabilities and those whose low receptive or expressive language skills make effective communication difficult, establishing informed consent requires attending to some specific issues. We pose some key questions that we think it important to reflect on as you plan your research and we provide some examples of how other researchers have addressed these issues.

Power and competing rights

Key question: Who has the power to give consent?

For a child or young person with SEND, should the decision-making power rest with the school, the parent, the child or young person with SEND or all of them? Assumptions are often made about the limited capacity of young children and those with learning disabilities to understand and therefore to give consent to participate in research (Bucknall, 2014; Cuskelly, 2005). This is why you will sometimes see the term *assent* used instead of *consent*. While *consent* refers to giving permission for something to happen, *assent* refers to the willingness to participate in research by someone who is deemed too young or lacking in capacity to give informed consent. In these cases, the parent or legal guardian gives consent and the child or young person gives assent. Whichever term you deem appropriate for your research, one complication that may arise is that of competing rights. As highlighted in Taylor's video clip, respecting a child's right to have a voice and be actively involved in matters which concern them, as enshrined in the UNCRC (1989), may conflict with a parent's right (and indeed, responsibility) to protect their child. There may be situations where a child wants to participate in research but the parent does not consent because they are suspicious of possible exploitation or want to protect their child's learning or leisure time. Equally, a parent may consent to their child being involved in research because of a perceived benefit, but the child does not wish to participate. Additionally, schools are viewed as being *in loco parentis* (Latin for 'in place of a parent') and therefore have some legal responsibilities for those in their care. Some schools interpret this as including being able to give consent for certain forms of research. Even if this is the case, we advocate an approach that supports fully informed consent for all of those who might be affected in some way by the research (school/institution staff, children and young people, and their parents and carers). As a general rule of thumb, we suggest obtaining consent from schools and parents/carers first – but making it clear that the consent of the child or young person is important to you as a researcher and that the research will therefore not proceed without it.

Capacity

Key question: How can you be sure that the child or young person with SEND understands what they are consenting to?

The cognitive functioning of a child with a learning or communication disability will almost certainly have been assessed using one or more psychometric instruments. Commonly used examples in the UK are the British Ability Scales, the Wechsler Intelligence Scale for Children and the British Picture Vocabulary Test. These norm-referenced instruments give a measure of a learner's cognitive and language functioning relative to others of the same age. One question that arises in relation to such assessments is whether a low 'mental age' or low receptive or expressive language score necessarily means that capacity is so low that it invalidates a child or young person's ability to understand and be involved in research? There is growing evidence that children (even very young children), and those whose capacity to understand the research and consent process might be questioned, are indeed able to exercise choice about their participation in research when approached in ways that take account of developmental levels, capacities and communication preferences (Breathnach et al., 2018; Bucknall, 2014; Gray and Winter 2011; Mayne et al., 2017). We believe that the more relevant question for the researcher is: How can I be sure that consent is fully informed in the case of this specific child or young person in this specific context? As Kellett (2005) points out, capacity to understand what a study involves will depend to a large extent on the vocabulary and methods used to explain it. We offer some practical examples later in the chapter.

Acquiescence

Key question: How can you be sure that the child or young person with SEND understands that their participation is voluntary and that they can stop participating if they change their mind?

The ethical principle of treating research participants with respect implies the need to avoid any form of coercion. This underpins the expectation that consent is fully informed and willingly given. But what about the possibility of acquiescence? This refers to someone agreeing to something but not because they really want to. The power differential between adults and children means that pupils in schools are generally accustomed to complying with adult requests (Graham et al., 2013; Scott-Barrett et al., 2019). This issue is particularly relevant to younger participants who may not want to disappoint a parent or a researcher by choosing not to participate in a project. Cuskelly (2005) suggests that acquiescence is also a potential issue when working with those with learning disabilities because they have a tendency to acquiesce and to respond 'yes' when asked a question. This means that a researcher could get an affirmative response to a question about willingness to participate in a project, or about understanding what is involved, even if the participant isn't sure if they want to participate or doesn't fully understand what they are agreeing to. Verbal explanations and accompanying visual supports need to be carefully planned to maximise understanding and minimise the possibility of an acquiescent response. Attending to body language may also alert the researcher to signs of acquiescence or a desire to withdraw from research activities.

The two examples below illustrate different ways that researchers sought consent in research involving young children. They also demonstrate their understandings of consent-seeking as an ongoing process that addresses the questions raised above.

Example 1

Breathnach et al. (2018) used a two-stage approach to gain parent and child consent for their research with five-year-old children in an Australian school. Stage one involved providing information and obtaining written consent from parents. Stage two involved a separate form that used child-friendly text and images to help explain the study. Parents were asked to read this with their children and then children were invited to write their name or make their mark on the form if they wished to participate. As the research took place over several school visits, the researchers made a point of verbally checking children's willingness to continue with the research and reminding them that they could choose not to participate at any time. Importantly, they also attended to non-verbal cues such as facial expression, body posture and engagement levels that might indicate a desire to opt out.

Example 2

Consent as an ongoing process is also nicely illustrated by Harcourt's (2011) research with children aged three to six years. As was the case for the example above, the children had their own separate consent form. Discussions about the project and what it would involve took place over several sessions and the children agreed that writing 'OK' on their consent form would indicate their willingness to participate in the research. In this example, the children were asked to do this each time the researchers visited the setting. A different colour was used for each visit so that for any given day, it was easy to identify a child who no longer wished to participate. This arrangement also provided children with a tangible reminder that they could opt out at any point and gave the researcher confidence that children were genuinely interested in participating.

In both of the examples above, the researchers accommodated the fact that young children's cognitive capacity and literacy skills are still developing. They used child-friendly information sheets that incorporated pictures rather than just words. In Example 1, they also recruited parents' help to ensure that children understood what was being asked of them and to ascertain their willingness to be involved. The assent process was simplified – children indicated their assent by writing their name (for those who were able to) or 'OK' or by making their special mark. In these examples, the key 'learner difference' that was accommodated was the children's age. But how might other differences be accommodated?

Activity 4.3

Accommodating learner differences

The examples above assume a level of manual dexterity, the ability to hold and manipulate a pencil or some other writing implement. But what if this is not the case, or if other learner differences impede effective communication. Respond to the two scenarios below. We have included our thoughts at the end of the chapter.

(Continued)

Scenario 1: Joshua is five years old and has cerebral palsy, which affects his manual dexterity skills to an extent that currently prohibits effective use of a writing implement. His cognitive abilities are in line with his chronological age. How might you enable him to indicate his assent or dissent to participate in the research examples above?

Scenario 2: Amy is six years old and has been profoundly deaf since birth. Although she wears hearing aids with a receiver and her teacher wears a transmitter, her audible range is extremely limited. Her lip-reading skills are developing and in class she, her teacher and some of her peers use limited amounts of British Sign Language (BSL) alongside their verbal communication. How might you enable Amy to understand and indicate her assent or dissent to participate in the research examples above?

Supporting informed consent

The suggestions below aim to support the informed consent process when research involves the direct participation of children and young people with SEND. The appropriateness of each will depend on the abilities and communication preferences of each learner. However, notice that strategies designed to support one group of learners will also support others. For example, an information sheet designed with minimal text in order to be accessible to pupils with learning disabilities will also support accessibility for pupils with hearing impairments, pupils whose first language is not English and pupils whose decoding skills are affected by dyslexia. This accords with Florian and Black-Hawkins' argument that inclusive educators move away from an approach that works with most learners (with something 'special' for the others) to one that is 'sufficiently available to everyone' (2011: 826).

- Adopt a multisensory approach and accompany any verbal explanation of the research with a physical information sheet.
- Clarity will maximise accessibility. Use simple language that participants will understand, keep written text to a minimum, use pictures, symbols and diagrams to support the text, and set the information out in a way that is easy to follow.
- Get creative. A leaflet, booklet, poster, diagram or cartoon are alternatives to a more traditional information sheet.
- Spending time in the setting observing what works for particular individuals will help you design an effective information sharing process.
- Pilot-test early drafts of an information sheet with pupils or seek feedback from those who know potential participants well, such as parents or teachers.
- Check understanding by asking participants to explain the project to someone else (a classmate, teaching assistant or parent).
- Consider seeking the assistance of someone who works closely with the child or young person and is therefore better able to communicate with them and ascertain what they understand about the project and whether or not they want to be involved.

- One student used a puppet to check what the pupils in her study understood. The puppet had not been present during the researcher's initial explanation. As a 'newcomer', the puppet was able to seek information from the pupils in a fun and informal way.
- Ensure that multiple opportunities are provided for prospective participants to ask questions.
- Attend to non-verbal communication. Facial expressions, gestures and levels of engagement can provide a useful check that a child or young person understands and is a willing participant.

Case study 4.1

Over the course of her degree, Lana had been volunteering in a learning support unit attached to a mainstream secondary school. The unit catered mainly for students with learning disabilities, some of whom also had ASD. As part of her Year 3 research project, Lana wanted to explore students' views and experiences of physical education. When considering how to ensure that student participation was as informed as possible, Lana reflected on what she had learned about the students and their learning environment over her time with them. She knew, for example, that the unit adopted a multisensory approach to teaching and learning and that visual supports were commonly used to aid communication. She also knew that some students had short attention spans and limited capacity to remember detailed information.

Lana chose to use a PowerPoint presentation to accompany the verbal explanation of her project. The presentation was short (just seven slides) and each slide contained small amounts of simple text supported by pictures and symbols. Lana sought feedback about her PowerPoint slides from the unit's learning support assistant and made some minor changes as a result. At the end of the presentation, Lana provided each student with their own colour printed copy to refer back to if they needed to. An enlarged copy was also displayed on the pupils' classroom wall. The students had several days to consider the information before their consent was formally sought.

Visual data and the protection of privacy

Key question: How can you ensure the protection of privacy when employing visual data-collection methods?

Innovative data-collection methods are increasingly being used in research involving children and those whose cognitive capacity or communication abilities limit the use of more traditional methods. In cases where data takes visual forms, providing anonymity can be more challenging (Wall, 2017). Photographs or video clips that include people or places, even in the distance, may reveal the identity of people or settings. Similarly, photographs of a pupil's work, drawing or construction may include details that make them identifiable. Where research outputs (your thesis, dissertation or a presentation of your research) includes visual data, it is therefore important that any features that might make people or places identifiable are either not included or are modified in such a way that this possibility is eliminated.

Example 1

Dunne et al. (2018) were interested in exploring how pupils and educators understood the concept of inclusion. Their study comprised two parts. In part 1, children and young people in special and mainstream schools took photos in their settings that they thought represented either inclusion or exclusion and then explained their choices to the researchers. In part 2, some of the photos and comments were shown to a range of educational professionals outside of the settings as a way of stimulating discussion about the concept of inclusion. This raised the issue of how to ensure that none of the participants in part 1 could be identified by the participants in part 2 or indeed by anyone who subsequently read the research report. In this project, the images were anonymised via software that 'cartoonised' them. This meant that although people within the individual settings might be able to recognise themselves and each other, no-one else would be able to. The researchers would also have taken care to select only those photos that did not include specific features that would have enabled an outsider to identify a school or individual. It is worth noting that when using visual research methods such as this, researchers in school settings would also be expected to approach the school's safeguarding officer to identify any pupils who are not to be photographed for child protection reasons.

Example 2

In her research on children's views about parental employment, Pimlott-Wilson (2012) used 'rainbows and clouds' as one of her data-collection methods. In one-to-one sessions with the researcher, the children used a 'rainbow' sheet to record their ideas (words and/or pictures) about positive aspects of parental employment and the 'clouds' sheet for perceived negative aspects. This method therefore produced physical artefacts, large sheets of paper with the children's work. The author notes that visual research methods like this mean that issues related to ownership and anonymity require careful consideration.

Activity 4.4

Ownership and privacy

Before reading on, consider your responses to the questions below:

1 Who 'owns' the children's creations, and who should keep them (the researcher, the school, the children)?
2 If the children's creations are 'borrowed' and then returned to them, how might this be done in a way that protects their privacy and provides anonymity?

What the researcher did

The children's creations, with their permission, were taken away and photographed so that the researcher could refer back to them for her analysis. She asked each child if they wanted their work returned to them. Some elected to have their work returned while others chose not to. The researcher notes that the children who chose not to retain their work indicated that their parents/carers may not have been pleased with some of what they had produced because it reflected negative feelings that may not have been discussed at home. Even though parents had consented to the research, this arrangement respected children's rights to their privacy and offered some ownership and control in the research process. Those children who wanted to retain their work received it in an individual sealed tube at the end of the school day, thus also protecting their privacy within the school setting.

Research ethics and power

Earlier in this chapter we drew attention to decision-making power in relation to the consent-seeking process. Power issues pervade the research process yet remain poorly acknowledged in much research. Feminist, indigenous and disability researchers have contributed much to our understanding of the many ways in which power impacts the research process and the potential of research to be exploitative or disabling. We noted in Chapter 1, for example, that much past research on disabled people took a pathological view and that those with disabilities were consequently represented as deviant or deficient. Even today, representations of those with various forms of SEND typically focus on the individual whereby they are represented as lacking, vulnerable and needing support. Additionally, learners ascribed particular labels are often thought about as a homogenous group. Such representations draw attention away from the broader, systemic contributors to poorer educational outcomes for some groups, and fail to adequately represent the abilities, strengths and resilience that individuals might demonstrate. They also contribute little to our understanding of the lived experiences of those with SEND. Examining power dynamics in research is therefore an ethical issue. Reflecting on who makes decisions about which research questions will be pursued, which data-collection methods and processes of analysis will be used, what form research outputs take, and how accessible these are to those who have enabled the research, are therefore important. They reveal where the balance of power lies, who benefits from the research and what impact this has on those who are the focus of the research. Examining power dynamics also provides opportunities to take steps to redress power imbalances. While we don't have the space to discuss these questions in this book, we suggest that participatory and inclusive approaches have much to offer in this regard and subsequent chapters will include some practical examples of how power differentials might be addressed when gathering and analysing data. These support the ethical principle of respect and contribute to more robust research outcomes.

Expect the unexpected

Ethical decisions will present themselves during the research process, sometimes in ways that the researcher may not have anticipated. This sometimes results in having to make spur of the moment decisions. This point in nicely illustrated in McNaughton and Smith's (2005) research on how Barbie influenced the identity constructions of three- to five-year-olds. The authors recount that one child had her own ideas about what she wanted to talk about rather than what the researcher wanted her to talk about. The researcher chose to follow the child's agenda rather than her own. Despite not being focused on Barbie, the conversation and the accompanying pictures drawn by the child produced some interesting and valuable data. As was the case for the other children, the researcher asked if she could keep this work to reflect on further and to share with others. However, the child indicated that she wanted to take it home. This was disappointing for the researcher. When, at the end of the day, the child's mother asked if she could try to persuade her daughter to give the drawings to the researcher, the answer was 'no' because the researcher wanted to maintain her ethical integrity – in this case, respecting the child's right to ownership and control of her own data.

This example highlights questions of power; namely, whose agenda takes precedence and who owns (controls) the data? It also illustrates that the inevitable uncertainty at the beginning of a project is part of why some researchers view ethical engagement as a process that develops in practice. While you can never know in advance exactly how your research will play out in practice, being clear about your principles and how they might be applied will support ethical practice.

Chapter summary

This chapter has shown that while agreement on general ethical principles might appear straightforward, decisions about how to apply them in practice are much less so. This is particularly the case if your research involves the active participation of children and young people with SEND. Guidelines and codes of practice provide a useful starting point but it is how they are interpreted and applied in specific situations that will determine the extent to which research is ethical or otherwise. There is no simple recipe that can be unthinkingly followed. Instead, ethical research requires a genuine engagement with the process of reflecting on the issues inherent in a given piece of research. We have drawn attention to some commonly occurring issues and provided some examples of how other researchers have managed them. While there may be no perfect solution to resolving the inevitable dilemmas, a 'reflexive revisiting' (Bourke et al., 2017) of your choices and actions throughout the research process will go some way to upholding the principle of respect that underpins all ethical research.

Checkpoint 4.1

Before proceeding with your research, you should be able to answer each of the questions below.

- How will you ensure that all participants are fully informed about the purpose of the research and what participation would involve?
- Who will you obtain consent from and how will you do so?
- How will you ensure that those who do not wish to participate in the research are able to communicate their dissent and to feel comfortable doing so?
- How will you be sure that participants understand that they can withdraw from the research and that they know how to do so?
- How will you provide anonymity or confidentiality? What are the limits of what you can offer in relation to these concepts and how will you communicate this to your participants?
- What costs or possible harms are there for participants and how can they be mitigated?
- How will you communicate findings to participants and convey that you value their contributions?

Our thoughts on 'Accommodating learner differences'

Scenario 1: Check what communication methods Joshua normally uses and use those. For example, could willingness or unwillingness to be involved in research be communicated verbally, non-verbally, using a sign and symbol system such as Makaton, or using technology such as a touchscreen showing assent and dissent faces or thumbs up and thumbs down icons. Joshua's teacher, classmates, parents/carers and, of course, Joshua himself could all help with this.

Scenario 2: In this instance, providing a suitable child-friendly written consent form, with pictures as well as words, will be particularly important given that the accompanying verbal explanation is less accessible to Amy than to her classmates. Seeking advice from Amy's teacher and parents/carers would also be important. They are used to communicating with her and will know what methods might work best in this instance. Their advice might include wearing the transmitter while you explain your research to the class, speaking at a moderate pace and enunciating carefully and ensuring that your face is clearly visible to Amy, and seeking the assistance of another BSL user to accompany your verbal explanation.

In both of these examples, attending to body language would also be an important way of checking what has been understood or what is being communicated.

Recommended reading

- Alderson, P. and Morrow, V. (2020) *The Ethics of Research with Children and Young People. A Practical Handbook.* London: Sage.

Overview: This book covers all stages of the research process but with a particular emphasis on ethical issues and the practicalities of managing them. We particularly recommend Chapters 7 and 8 for detailed coverage of ways to go about informing children about your research and seeking their consent.

- Graham, A., Powell, M., Taylor, N., Anderson, D. and Fitzgerald, R. (2013) *Ethical Research Involving Children.* Florence: UNICEF Office of Research – Innocenti.

Outline: This UNICEF compendium is the result of an international project. It brings together a range of views, guidance, case studies and thinking points aimed at helping researchers ensure that children's dignity, rights and well-being are respected in all research. It's a hefty volume (220 pages) but the table of contents enables readers to locate specific areas of interest. The downloadable pdf is free to use as long as the source is acknowledged. It is available at: https://tinyurl.com/y5zjc8ms

- The Norah Fry Research Centre

Outline: The Norah Fry Research Centre, based at the University of Bristol (England), specialises in undertaking research on (and with) people with learning disabilities. You will see that their *easy information* and *easy to read* research summaries report some of their research using large print, simplified language and accompanying illustrations as a way of making it more accessible to those with learning disabilities.
www.bristol.ac.uk/sps/research/centres/norahfryresearch

- Stanley Milgram's experiments

Outline: In this research, participants were required to administer increasingly powerful electric shocks to other (supposed) participants. The people supposedly receiving the electric shocks were in fact confederates of the researcher and were only pretending to be in pain. Milgram's research was subsequently heavily criticised for the deception and psychological distress caused to participants. The weblink takes you to a short YouTube clip that illustrates what the experiment involved and the distress it caused. See https://tinyurl.com/y3l7x7aw

---

5

REVIEWING THE LITERATURE IN SPECIAL AND INCLUSIVE EDUCATION

━━━━━━━━━━━ Chapter objectives ━━━━━━━━━━━

By the end of this chapter you will:

- ✓ Understand the main purposes of the literature review in research
- ✓ Be able to describe the key steps and tasks in undertaking a literature review
- ✓ Be able to identify appropriate sources of literature relevant to researching special educational needs and inclusion
- ✓ Understand what is meant by 'critical evaluation' of literature

Introduction

Chapter 3 highlighted the importance of familiarising yourself with literature relevant to your general area of interest as part of your planning process. It enables you to make informed decisions about what research questions are worthwhile and where your research would sit alongside that which has already been undertaken. Burton et al. (2014) distinguish between this initial search that takes place during the early planning phase of a study and the subsequent more detailed review that takes place once your research questions have been established. While the former is more like a scoping exercise, the latter requires a comprehensive and systematic approach that produces a structured argument and case for your own research. This chapter aims to guide you through that process.

What is a literature review?

First, let's look at how a literature review is defined in three widely read educational research texts. Each is a little longer and adds a little more detail. Together, they highlight some of the important features of a good literature review.

> A literature review is an account of what has been published on a topic by other researchers (Burton et al., 2014: 35).

> A review of the literature is a summary, analysis and interpretation of the theoretical, conceptual and research literature related to a topic or theme (Mutch, 2013: 90).

> A literature review is a critical analysis of what is understood already about your topic and themes related to it, and of some of the varied perspectives which have been expressed (Lambert, 2012: 80).

From these quotations, we can see that a good literature review is more than simply a summary of research about a particular topic. It is also an analysis and interpretation about that body of research. Additionally, the analysis needs to be 'critical' and the review should be balanced – in other words, include the full range of perspectives relevant to your topic. This last point is particularly pertinent to the field of special and inclusive education where views on topics can differ widely and where some issues remain hotly debated.

Commonly asked questions

Figure 5.1 presents some of the questions most frequently posed by our students in relation to their literature reviews. There are no standard answers to these questions as each literature review will be different depending on the specific topic and research questions. You will need to make a judgement about what is most appropriate for your particular research focus. This chapter will support you in making these judgements.

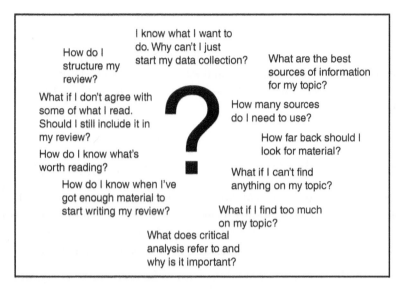

Figure 5.1 Commonly asked questions

What is the purpose of the literature review?

The literature review performs several interconnected functions in the research process.

First, it sets out the framework or context for your research. In our work with students we sometimes refer to this as 'setting the scene'. By highlighting how your research relates to the wider historical, social or political contexts relevant to your research, you start to make a case for why your research will be of interest to others.

Second, familiarising yourself with the literature related to your topic provides you with a solid understanding of what is currently known about your topic. This prevents unnecessary duplication of research and enables you to identify how your study contributes to what is already known. In our experience, students often become excited as they learn new things about their chosen topic. In some cases, this results in them seeing things from a different perspective, seeing connections that they had not previously been aware of, or even revising their research question in line with new learning. Reading widely as part of this familiarisation process will therefore leave you feeling more confident about the focus and direction of your research and the contribution it will make to the current state of knowledge.

As noted in Mutch's (2013) definition, the literature review needs to summarise what is currently known about your topic, but it needs to do so in a particular way. Specifically, a literature review needs to include *analysis* (breaking a text down to identify the different key points), *synthesis* (bringing ideas from different authors together) and *critique* (evaluating and comparing points made by different authors). It is these elements that differentiate a literature review from an annotated bibliography. While the latter resembles a list that simply describes and summarises the literature someone has read, the former identifies and explains how different ideas connect with each other, which aspects of a topic authors agree and disagree on, and which aspects remain under-researched. A literature review will also define key terms and explain key concepts or theoretical perspectives relevant to your research. It is in these ways that your literature review becomes a carefully crafted piece of writing that sets up an issue, question or problem that your research will address.

What is meant by 'criticality' and why is it important?

We noted above that one important difference between a literature review and an annotated bibliography is that the former includes an element of critical analysis while the latter does not. We often find that students have difficulty understanding criticality and how to incorporate it into their writing, so we offer the points below to help you with this.

Let's start with the word 'critical'. In everyday usage, this term implies negative judgement or a process that involves criticising something. In academic circles, however, it has a slightly different meaning, one that aligns more closely with the more neutral terms 'evaluate' or 'assess'. Critical analysis may, but does not necessarily, involve criticism or a negative judgement. It's more about providing a balanced consideration that recognises both the strengths and limitations of a piece of research or point of view. A critical analysis requires you to look carefully and to ask questions about what you read. These questions might relate to balance of argument, hidden assumptions, methodological soundness or quality of the evidence base.

There are several reasons why a critical analysis is an important element of a literature review. First, it is a way of acknowledging that all research takes place in contested terrain within which alternative views and positions exist. An example applicable to the field of inclusive education is the opposing views on the relative merits (or otherwise) of special schools. Some scholars are strong advocates for special schools, while others argue equally strongly against them. While this is a rather obvious example, the key point is that there will be differences of opinion about many topics relevant to special and inclusive education. A critical analysis will highlight the range of views found and ensure that your review offers a holistic and fair representation of them. It is often the case that important and valid points are made on both sides of an argument. A critical analysis will identify and evaluate them. This involves not taking what is written at face value but rather, looking closely to identify the beliefs, values or assumptions that underpin a particular piece of research or point of view, which may not be stated explicitly. Identifying them may help you to explain differences of opinion that you find in the literature you read. It is this sort of work that transforms a literature review from being a simple descriptive account to one that offers a carefully considered analysis and a personal response to what you have read.

Second, a critical analysis accepts that no research study will be perfect. Rather, each will have its strengths and limitations. They might be related to the methodological approach, the sample size, the data-collection methods chosen, or the way in which data is analysed, interpreted or presented. A critical analysis identifies these strengths and limitations and judges the research findings in light of them. Additionally, research outcomes (or how they are reported) can be one-sided or misleading due to researcher bias, vested interests or deliberate deceit. A critical analysis therefore also considers these possibilities when evaluating how much credence to give a particular study. You could use the questions presented in Table 5.1 to guide your critical analysis.

Example: All research has limitations

In her review of the influence of teaching assistants (TAs) on the learning of pupils identified with special educational needs, Saddler (2014) takes issue with Blatchford et al.'s (2012) research that found that pupils who received the most TA support made less progress than similar pupils who received no such support. This large and extended study meets many of the criteria normally used to assess research quality. Indeed, this project and its subsequent publications have produced much of value for schools wanting to improve the ways in which they deploy their TAs (Sharples et al., 2015). Nevertheless, Saddler's analysis makes some important points. She highlights, for example, that the poorer outcomes found for pupils with SEND in this research were based entirely on narrowly defined academic outcomes, as determined by a quantitative-based questionnaire. She raises the question of whether additional or different research outcomes would have resulted if the research had also included some qualitative case studies and incorporated the experiences and views of pupils with SEND themselves. She additionally highlights the strong relationship between academic success and social inclusion, and points out that the role of TAs in facilitating social inclusion of pupils with SEND (and by implication, academic success) was neglected in this research. This example of critical analysis illustrates that even high-quality research will inevitably have some limitations.

Example: Beware the lone wolf

Some of you will have heard of the research that claimed a link between the MMR (measles, mumps and rubella) vaccination and autism. It was published in *The Lancet*, a highly respected medical journal, and sparked a global debate about the safety of this widely used vaccine. It took many years for the full facts to emerge and for the researchers' arguments to be fully debunked. Deer's (2011) investigation found that the data had been misreported or altered in all 12 cases on which the conclusions were based. He also uncovered that participants were recruited through anti-MMR campaigners or were already of the opinion that the vaccination had caused their child's symptoms. This introduced a significant (and unacknowledged) bias into the sample selected for the study. Additionally (and again, unacknowledged), the principal investigator received significant financial reward for his research, which had been commissioned to support a lawsuit against the vaccine's manufacturers. In other words, he had a personal interest in a particular research outcome. It was a full decade before this research was formally retracted from *The Lancet*. While this is an extreme and thankfully rare example, it is nonetheless a pertinent reminder that even research published in one of the most highly regarded medical journals is not above scrutiny. We therefore concur with Thomas who argues that 'you should approach everything you read and hear with a questioning mind' (2017: 69). This is the crux of critical analysis.

Table 5.1 Questions that support critical analysis

Key questions	Sub-questions
Has the author summarised **the weight of evidence** in relation to different views on the topic?	Are all relevant areas of the topic covered or have some areas been ignored or marginalised?
	Are there other views on this topic that have not been acknowledged?
	Might the author have some vested interests in drawing particular conclusions?
	Has the work been published in a reputable source?
Has the author made **questionable assumptions**?	What assumptions, values or beliefs have not been explicitly stated but are nonetheless implied within the publication?
	What do you think about these? Are they reasonable or open to debate?
In the case of primary research, is it **methodologically sound**?	Has the author provided enough detail about the data-collection methods, sampling procedures and approach to analysis for you to make a judgement about the methodological quality of the research?
	Are these aspects of the research appropriate for the research questions posed?
	Might the researchers have arrived at different answers if they had done their research in a different way?
Do claims made in the publication match the **evidence provided**?	Are the conclusions logical and credible?
	Has sufficient evidence been provided to convince you of the conclusions drawn or the arguments made?
	Could alternative conclusions be drawn from the evidence gathered?

Activity 5.1

Comparing papers

Select two journal articles that report primary research relevant to your topic and critically compare them. Use the questions in Table 5.1 and the framework in Table 5.2 to guide your comparison. Remember that critical analysis is not primarily about criticising; rather, it involves a thoughtful evaluation that identifies the strengths as well as the limitations inherent in any research project.

Table 5.2   Framework for comparing papers

	Paper 1	Paper 2
Research design and justification (methodology)		
Selection procedures for participation (sampling)		
Data-collection procedures (methods)		
Data-quality procedures (trustworthiness, credibility)		
Data management and analysis (analysis techniques, data storage)		
Other noteworthy points		

Overview of the literature review process

If this is your first literature review, you may feel unsure about where and how to start. It can be helpful to see your literature review as a three-stage process, each involving a number of key tasks. First you need to search for and access appropriate literature. Once you have gathered your material, you need to read and digest it. Finally comes the task of writing and structuring your review. We summarise key tasks in Figure 5.2 before discussing some elements in more detail.

Search and sort

A range of sources

For any given topic, there is a wide range of potentially useful sources of literature.

Each category has some strengths and limitations. For a balanced review, we recommend including material from a range of different categories.

Authored books (where the whole book has been written by one or more authors) are likely to offer extended coverage of a particular topic but finding one dedicated to your exact research question is unlikely (Thomas, 2017). An **edited book** (where

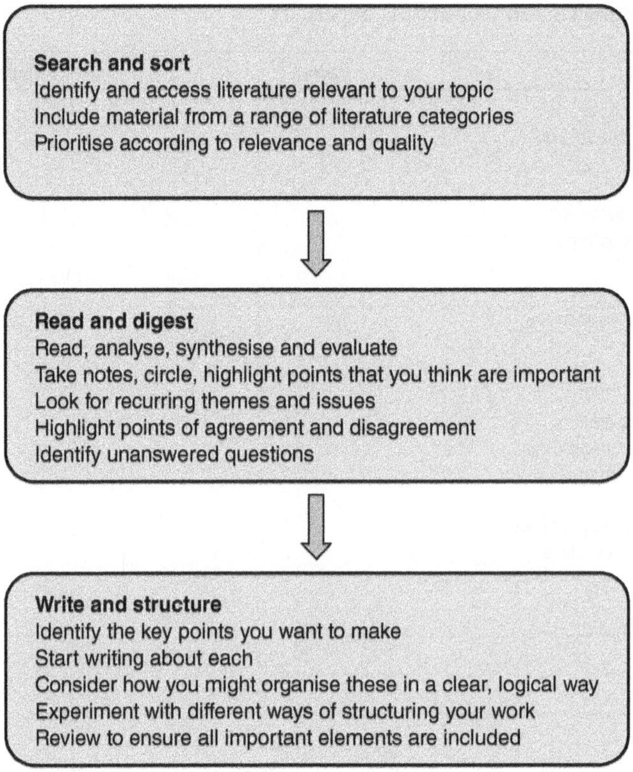

Search and sort
Identify and access literature relevant to your topic
Include material from a range of literature categories
Prioritise according to relevance and quality

Read and digest
Read, analyse, synthesise and evaluate
Take notes, circle, highlight points that you think are important
Look for recurring themes and issues
Highlight points of agreement and disagreement
Identify unanswered questions

Write and structure
Identify the key points you want to make
Start writing about each
Consider how you might organise these in a clear, logical way
Experiment with different ways of structuring your work
Review to ensure all important elements are included

Figure 5.2 Overview of the literature review process

each chapter is written by a different author but all chapters focus on a broad common theme), may well have some chapters that relate more directly to your research question. Be aware that the timeframe for producing a book normally stretches across several years. This means that by the time a book is published, some content may be outdated or less relevant. Nevertheless, books should always be considered an important source.

Journal articles report the very latest research. They are much shorter than a book and therefore less time-consuming to read, and they tend to have a very specific focus. This means that in comparison to a book, you are more likely to find a journal article that is directly relevant to your research question. Peer-reviewed journal articles have the added advantage of having been carefully scrutinised by other researchers working in the same field. This generally makes them an important and reliable source of information for all research projects. However, many journal articles assume specialised knowledge amongst their readership (Thomas, 2017). This makes them less accessible to the general public, or indeed, research students. At the end of the chapter we provide a short list of some of the journals that our students have found accessible (easy to read and digest) and relevant to their chosen topics. Finally, look out for **special issues**, in which an entire issue of a journal is dedicated to a specific topic. Finding a special issue relevant to your topic is like finding a large gold nugget!

Unpublished theses or dissertations, which you can access via your university's institutional repository, are also well worth a look. This is where you may find something on a topic very similar to your own. However, bear in mind that these research projects are unpublished and therefore have not been peer-reviewed for quality. Similarly, we recommend that you avoid relying heavily on **general internet searches** to find material on your topic. Well-known search engines may provide some useful sources but they must be carefully evaluated for credibility and quality of information.

Government departments offer another potentially useful source of information. Documents such as official policies and statistical releases are usually free to download and may provide some important background information for your project. Analysis of such documents may also reveal a need for additional information and be used to justify your chosen topic. Recall Scott from Chapter 3. He became interested in the relationship between school exclusions and pupils with SEND after reading the *Guardian* headline 'Thousands of children with special needs excluded from school'. He was able to verify this claim by checking the latest Department for Education statistical release on school exclusions. However, his search also revealed that there was no breakdown of these statistics according to SEND. There was therefore no way of verifying his anecdotal evidence that it was pupils with ASD who were disproportionately represented in the exclusion statistics. He saw this as an important oversight and an area that would benefit from further investigation.

Many **non-governmental organisations** (NGOs) also provide free access to some excellent information or resources. There are many examples that our students have found useful including the Centre for Studies on Inclusive Education, Leonard Cheshire Disability, the National Autistic Society, the National Children's Bureau and World of Inclusion. Some organisations also publish their own research reports but bear in mind that these have not been peer-reviewed in the same way that journal articles are and therefore should be carefully assessed for balance and quality. Various forms of **mass media**, both traditional and non-traditional, could also be considered. Newspaper and magazine articles, television and radio broadcasts, YouTube clips, podcasts and blogs may all stimulate your thinking or provide evidence for a particular point of view. Again, caution needs to be exercised with each source being evaluated for quality and credibility.

When you find a publication that is particularly relevant to your topic, don't forget to check the **reference list** for other items that may be useful. **Recommended reading lists** at the end of book chapters may also offer valuable sources. Finally, don't forget to talk to others. Your module or course tutor, relevant professionals, your supervisor, and also colleagues and classmates may have some useful knowledge or recommendations about sources. This was the case for one of our students who wanted to investigate images of disability through the media over time. A tutor mentioned a publication by well-known disability activist Richard Rieser. A relatively short search found Rieser's publication *Disabling Imagery*, which was free to download from the British Film Institute website. It proved to be an excellent source which guided some of her research decisions.

Use technology

New technologies mean that identifying specific books, journal articles and other sources of information relevant to your topic is much easier today than in the past. All universities and many public libraries subscribe to a range of searchable electronic databases. The Web of Science and Zetoc are two well-known generic databases but we recommend using one or more of the subject-specific databases. The British Educational Index (BEI), Education Resources Information Centre (ERIC), Australian Education Index (AEI) and PsycINFO are four databases that our students have found particularly useful. Note that all the databases and many journals allow you to set up alerts that will inform you of any new publications identified by your search terms. This is a useful way of keeping up to date with the latest research on your topic.

Effective use of search functions will involve an element of trial and error as you experiment with different search terms to find what works best for your particular topic. It will also require familiarising yourself with how to use Boolean operators to broaden and limit your search. We intentionally don't cover these skills in this chapter as they are well covered in many other research texts, but you can find a useful overview of what Boolean operators are and how to use them from the Open University resource featured in our Recommended reading at the end of the chapter.

It is likely that your initial key search terms will produce either too many or too few results. Too many results makes it time-consuming to read everything and to identify the best items for your review. In this case, you need to apply one or more exclusion criteria. Common examples are: date of publication (prioritise more recent publications over older ones); location of the research (national or international); type of setting (special or mainstream); and phase of education (early years, primary, secondary, tertiary). With regard to date of publication, bear in mind that there will be some seminal publications that remain important even if published some time ago. You may also need to include some older publications as part of providing some historical context to your research.

If your search produces too few results, you may not have enough material to write your review. It may also indicate that your search terms have missed potentially important publications. Additionally, the specific nature of a good research question means that you are unlikely to find books or journal articles on your exact research question. This is why it is often useful to broaden your search to include areas that are related but not necessarily specific to your research question. You could do this by expanding the age range, the SEND range, the type of setting, the country in which the research took place, or by making the focus of your search less specific. The two examples below illustrate how our students have applied these ideas.

╭─ **Case study 5.1** ─────────────────────────────────

Example 1

In Chapter 3 you met Taya whose initial research question was 'How can schools promote the inclusion of pupils with ASD?' She needed to re-work this very broad question into one with a much sharper focus that was more feasible within the scope of a Year 3 dissertation. To do this she applied the following criteria: type of setting; age of learner; and focus of learning. This produced the more manageable research question, 'What strategies and resources can support the communication skills of Key Stage 1 children with ASD who attend a mainstream school?' When she searched for relevant literature she used these same criteria to limit the massive number of publications related to 'inclusion' and 'ASD' that she initially found. She subsequently further reduced the total number of items by eliminating literature published more than ten years ago and by prioritising research undertaken in the same national context. This resulted in a more manageable set of publications with which to proceed with her review.

Example 2

Kiran had spent her Year 2 placement in a special school that catered primarily for learners with ASD. During her time there, some of the children visited a nearby farm that offered animal therapy. They appeared to benefit from these visits and this sparked Kiran's interest in the potential value of animal therapy. She decided that her Year 3 dissertation would investigate the impact of animal therapy on primary school children with ASD. Kiran's initial search found very little on that specific topic. She needed to broaden her focus and search terms. Instead of searching just for 'animal therapy', she widened her search to include 'alternative therapies' and 'non-traditional therapies'. She also removed the age and type of SEND limiters that she had applied to her initial search.

Kiran's broader search identified articles on animal-assisted interaction (AAI). All of them involved adults and took a health focus. Nevertheless, they provided some indication of healthcare benefits of AAI across a range of settings, populations and conditions. She also found articles on 'pet therapy', 'play therapy', 'music therapy' and 'drama therapy' that supported the potential value of non-traditional therapies for children. Further refining of her search terms located two articles on AAI which related specifically to adults with ASD as well as a systematic review (see Chapter 6) of AAI with adults. Together, these materials provided a good starting point for her review.

Start broad then narrow down

Earlier in the chapter we highlighted that one purpose of a literature review is to make a case for why your research will be of interest to others. This means that your review will focus not only on your specific research topic but also on the broader context within which it is located. This is one reason why we recommend the 'start broad and then narrow down' approach illustrated in Figure 5.3. Additionally, there is likely to be a lot of literature relevant to the general area of your research, less on the specific area you want to investigate, and even less on your exact research question. Your literature review needs to bring together relevant points from across these levels so that even if there is very little published research on your exact topic, you have enough material to support the arguments you want to make. In the example above, Kiran found that publications on a range of non-traditional therapies and across a range of populations provided a relevant context for her specific focus on AAI and children with ASD.

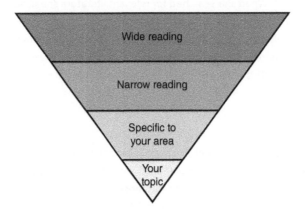

Figure 5.3   Start broad then narrow down

Read and digest

Read selectively

Most projects will have time constraints to which you must adhere. This means that once you have found a good range of material, you need to be selective about what you read. This requires identifying what is most relevant to your specific project. Reading introductions, headings, subheadings and conclusions will provide a good indication of a publication's likely relevance to your project. In the case of journal articles, read the abstract. For reports, read the executive summary. For books, use chapter titles and the index to help locate information that is relevant to your study. Your aim is to eliminate less relevant material.

Some academics distinguish between skimming and scanning. Skimming refers to a quick glance through a publication to get a general feel for content while scanning refers to a slightly slower process that involves looking for specific information such as key words or concepts. You will need to use both of these speed-reading skills as part of your selective reading process. Consider rating each item using a 1–5 scale where 1 represents not at all relevant to your project and 5 represents extremely relevant. You can then prioritise those items with the highest ratings.

Keep track of what you read

A complete and accurate reference list at the end of your dissertation or thesis is an important academic convention. It allows readers to access any publications cited in your work that may be of particular interest to them – just in the way that you might follow up on some of the sources that you find in the literature you read as part of your search process. This means recording all relevant bibliographic details of everything you read.

There are various ways of doing this. Some students keep their own cumulative lists and summaries, either electronic or handwritten. Others use a template system to record important details of what they read. Yet others use one of the commercially available referencing management systems such as Endnote or Refworks. You will need to decide what works best for you and what is most appropriate for your situation. For large projects such as a doctoral or master's thesis, the initial investment of time to familiarise yourself with Endnote or Refworks will pay dividends. For smaller projects, consider using a template. A template offers a set of prompts for summarising and categorising each item you read. You could use or adapt the example we provide at the end of this chapter (see Table 5.3).

Write and structure

Once you have completed the bulk of your reading, it is time to begin writing and structuring your review. By this time, you will already have some clear ideas about what is currently understood about your topic as well as what some of the key issues and unanswered questions are. You will have also identified points of agreement and disagreement between authors and identified gaps in the research base. Your next task is to present this to the reader in a clear and logical way. There is no single correct way of structuring your work but an organising technique may help with this. In Chapter 3 we showed how a mindmap or spider diagram offers a useful way of collating thoughts as you refine your research question. The same techniques can be used to guide the structure of your literature review. Your research aims and questions may provide some guide as to what subheadings might be useful to structure your work. Alternatively, grouping ideas thematically is another common way of coming up with a logical framework. Be patient and remember that you may need to re-work your structure several times before you are satisfied with the final result.

Chapter summary

This chapter has looked at the role of the literature review in the research process and has offered guidance on how you might approach this part of your study. We have highlighted a number of key elements and emphasised the importance of analysis, synthesis and critique in achieving these. By the end of your review, you should be able to answer 'yes' to each item in checkpoint 5.1.

Checkpoint 5.1

- The review is based on wide reading and includes a range of sources.
- The review provides a fair and balanced representation of the range of perspectives found about your topic.
- Key themes, trends and points of agreement are identified.
- Key issues, debates and areas of controversy are identified.
- Literature cited is critically evaluated.
- The review clarifies links between the research question and broader contexts.
- The review supports a case for your proposed research.
- The review has a clear, logical structure.

Table 5.3 Example template for tracking literature read

Reference	(Title, author, editor if chapter in edited book, date, source, URL)
Type of publication	(Empirical research, policy, opinion piece, review article)
If research-based …	(Research aims, methods, location, sample, key findings and conclusions)
Key ideas, issues and arguments	(Summary of key findings or arguments)
Critical comments	(Evaluation of quality, strengths, limitations)
Relevance to research question	(How does it connect to my research?)
Additional comments	

Recommended reading

- Chapter 3 in Thomas, G. (2017) *How to Do Your Research Project: A Guide for Students.* London: Sage.

Outline: This chapter expands on some of the ideas presented here but provides additional content on speed reading, note-taking and referencing. It is written in an engaging and accessible way and the examples used to illustrate points take an educational focus.

- Fink, A. (2019) *Conducting Research Literature Reviews. From Internet to Paper.* London: Sage.

Outline: This book provides in-depth coverage of how to conduct a literature review. It is written for a general academic audience rather than education or social science scholars in particular but it includes useful examples that illustrate the concepts and processes that are presented.

- Hart, C. (2018) *Doing a Literature Review. Releasing the Research Imagination.* London: Sage.

Outline: This book is also dedicated entirely to the literature review process. It is part of the SAGE Study Skills series and includes extended examples that illustrate how techniques and processes can be applied.

- The Open University (UK) www.open.ac.uk/library/services/advanced-searching

Outline: This free, printable resource provides succinct coverage of some useful searching techniques: identifying the best key words, phrase-searching; Boolean logic, truncation, wildcards and common pitfalls.

Journals that our students have found particularly useful for their research projects:

- *British Journal of Special Education*
- *Education Review*
- *European Journal of Special Needs Education*
- *International Journal of Inclusive Education*
- *International Journal of Early Childhood Special Education*
- *Journal of International Special Needs Education*
- *Learning Disability Quarterly*
- *Review of Educational Research*
- *Support for Learning*
- *Teacher Education and Special Education*

6

COMMON METHODOLOGICAL APPROACHES IN SPECIAL AND INCLUSIVE EDUCATIONAL RESEARCH

================ Chapter objectives ================

By the end of this chapter you will:

✓ Know the key features associated with four common methodological approaches in special and inclusive education
✓ Be able to highlight the positives and drawbacks associated with each of the four approaches
✓ Understand the ways in which your ontological and epistemological views shape the methodological approaches you select
✓ Be able to identify one/multiple methodological approaches that could be appropriate in meeting your research aims

---

Introduction

This chapter aims to explore some common methodological approaches to undertaking research in special and inclusive education; it will highlight the intrinsic features of four distinct approaches. Additionally, innovative approaches will be explored in Chapter 9 and the methods that may accompany these approaches are presented in Chapters 7 and 8. At this point, it is useful to remind yourself of the thinking process that was introduced in Chapter 2 and outlined in Figure 6.1.

Figure 6.1   Thinking process for identifying paradigms

We explored ontological and epistemological viewpoints in Chapter 2, and how to go about ethically designing your research project in Chapters 3 to 5. In this chapter, we move further along the process of thinking to enable you to determine which common methodological approach may be most suitable for your research project in special and inclusive education. You will usually choose just one approach to follow in a given study. However, it is important that you familiarise yourself with a range of approaches so that you are making the best choice for your particular research aims. The approaches explored in this chapter include:

- Case study
- Action research
- Systematic review of the literature
- Mixed methods

Introducing key terms for this chapter
Methodological approach

By 'methodological approach' we mean the area of thinking that refers specifically to the procedure that will be followed to gather and analyse data in a given study. Note the difference here between 'methodology' and 'methodological approach'. Methodology can be best explained by conceptualising it as the entire process reflected in Figure 6.1. Methodological approach, however, is only one part of this process; it refers to the specific strategy that is used to sample and gather data in your study (Cohen et al., 2018).

To help further with this distinction, it may be useful for you to reflect on the still very relevant words of Sartori (1970):

Most of the literature introduced by the title 'Methods' (in the social, behavioural or political sciences) actually deals with survey techniques and social statistics, and has little if anything to share with the crucial concern of 'methodology,' which is a concern with the logical structure and procedure of scientific enquiry. In a very crucial sense there is no methodology without *logos*, without thinking about thinking. And if a firm distinction is drawn – as it should be – between methodology and technique, the latter is no substitute for the former. One may be a wonderful researcher and manipulator of data, and yet remain an unconscious thinker (p.1033).

We are aware that the nuances in defining these separate terms can be difficult to get your head around. However, spending time navigating them can result in a stronger study and write-up, particularly at the highest level of study (doctoral level). We are also aware that different authors define these terms in different ways, and that can be exceptionally confusing for a student trying to develop an understanding of them. Therefore, to help you through the fog of these complex terms as you are reading, try to continually reflect upon the following:

- Your research question and aims must be the main driver of the research approach and methods that you choose to undertake.
- Always ask yourself these three questions: 1) Is what I am planning to do appropriate in meeting the aims of my study? 2) Will I gather relevant data? 3) Will my data answer my research question?

Empirical

An empirical study can be conceptualised as one that is carried out 'in the field of research'. Therefore, empirical research usually involves live participants from whom data can be gathered – via observations, questionnaires or interviews, for example. Empirical research in special and inclusive education is often undertaken in educational settings, such as schools or colleges. We find that the majority of students undertaking a study in special and inclusive education elect to undertake an empirical study.

Non-empirical

A non-empirical study denotes a study that uses secondary data to meet its research aims. Therefore, unlike empirical studies, no data are gathered from live participants in the field of research. Common sources of secondary data include numerical data sets and published research from other authors. This approach is most often used when the aims of a given study have a strong theoretical focus. Examples of common empirical and non-empirical methodological approaches are explored in this chapter and later in Chapter 9.

Approach 1: Case study

The case study is one of the most common methodological approaches used by students in the field of special and inclusive education in meeting their research aims. A useful core text in navigating the details associated with the case study approach is:

Yin, R.K. (2018) *Case Study Research and Applications.* London: Sage.

The case study methodological approach can be defined as 'a strategy for doing research which involves an empirical investigation of a particular contemporary phenomenon within its real life context using multiple sources of evidence' (Robson, 2002: 178). Thus, the case study is an empirical study, as data are gathered 'in the field' via a range of collection methods. These data-collection methods may include interviews, observations, questionnaires/surveys or other forms of typically talk/discussion-based methods. Well-designed case studies usually employ more than one of these data-collection methods, which will be explored in much greater detail in Chapters 7 and 8.

The key feature that makes a case study approach different from other empirical approaches is that it takes place within a 'bounded system'. To translate this to studies in special and inclusive education, the 'bounded system' tends to be a particular educational setting, for example a school or a university course group. Case studies are, therefore, a helpful approach to employ if you wish to explore the relationships between different phenomena in a very specific context. Students in special and inclusive education who are studying or working in a particular school, for example, are often motivated to develop a deeper understanding in relation to a particular aspect of that context and choose a case study approach in which to do so. The 'bounded system' could also be an individual educator or learner. However, there are significant ethical considerations related to conducting research about/with one person, so an interest in research related to an individual should be discussed at length with your supervisor. To help you conceptualise the topics that are well studied using a case study approach, an example of a prior case study is given below from research that we have supervised.

Case study 6.1

Jasmine worked as a higher level teaching assistant (HLTA) in an inclusion unit attached to a mainstream secondary school. The students that she supported were often deemed to have displayed problematic behaviour that resulted in them being excluded from the mainstream part of the school. Many of the learners who found themselves in the inclusion unit had a diagnosis of ADHD. Jasmine wanted to investigate the link between ADHD diagnosis and being educated in the inclusion unit, with the aim of better understanding how these students could be supported to reach their educational potential. The case study approach was the most appropriate for Jasmine in effectively meeting her research aims. The study took place within a bounded system, her school; she undertook interviews with a range of teaching staff and learners. These interviews allowed Jasmine to identify some common characteristics to the learners' journeys, which helped the teaching staff to better understand inclusive pedagogy in their context.

Positives and drawbacks of the case study approach

The strongest criticism levelled at the case study approach could be argued to be its most significant strength. It can be argued that the case study approach has very limited generalisability due to the context specificity of the data gathered. By 'generalisability' we mean the ability for the conclusions drawn from a study to translate to other contexts; for example, for the conclusions drawn about behaviour management techniques in one school to be relevant in another school, or a range of schools.

However, many believe that successful school-based research involves developing understanding about 'a school', thereby increasing our understanding of 'other schools' and this has the potential to contribute to our collective knowledge about 'The School' (Simons, 2009). Claims of low generalisability are often made by researchers who view the case study as the study of a single phenomenon rather than a methodological approach or a research strategy. It can be argued that understanding the subtlety and complexity of an individual case is its strength and the 'force of example' that it provides can, for some researchers, be as useful as a large-scale comparative study (Flyvbjerg, 2006). Indeed, it could be argued that many settings in special and inclusive education have elements that are unique due to the specificity of the education that they provide. Therefore, generalisability may not be a particularly useful goal for those researching in this area.

Conclusively, it is perfectly feasible to follow an interest in exploring an aspect of theory/ practice in only one school as long as you plan and execute the study effectively; this can be just as valid to educational theory as a large-scale, multi-school approach. Additionally, if you are studying at undergraduate or master's level, you often may not have the time to explore multiple settings and it is important that you are not overly ambitious with your study. It is always better to undertake smaller-scale research of strong academic rigour rather than plan something too ambitious and reduce the overall quality of your research.

Checkpoint 6.1

- A case study involves undertaking research in one specific context (often a school/ college/group) using multiple data-collection methods.
- It involves empirical research. Therefore, you must gather data in the setting with 'live' participants.
- This approach is worth considering if you are interested in exploring a specific educational phenomenon in one context.

A note on the multiple case study approach

The multiple case study approach is often employed by students who wish to explore a particular educational phenomenon across multiple contexts – for example, across three different special schools. This approach can support a higher level of generalisability, as the conclusions drawn pertain to multiple settings rather than one, as with the single case study design. However, it should be noted that multiple case studies are often very time and resource intensive as the data-collection process needs to be replicated across multiple settings. Therefore, it is often recommended to students who have a long timescale for research completion, usually those at doctoral level. For more information on the multiple case study approach consult the recommended core text by Yin (2018).

Approach 2: Action research

The action research approach is also empirical in nature, meaning that it involves gathering data 'in the field'. Similar in nature to the case study approach, action research is often selected by students who wish to explore a particular educational phenomenon in a specific context. It is particularly useful for students who work in educational settings and wish to gain a deeper understanding related to an issue they may have identified, with the aim of improving practice. The statement by Durcikova et al. (2018: 24) is helpful in conceptualising the defining feature of action research, that: 'In action research, the action and the research work hand-in-hand. Neither the action nor the research may be properly planned, conducted, or evaluated separately from the other.'

As the quotation highlights, the main difference between the case study approach and the action research approach is that, in action research, the research takes place alongside taking action to change practice. To give an example, you may have identified in your educational setting that learners with ASD are not reaching their potential in maths. As well as researching why that may be, you also want to make changes to your practice to try and support those learners to reach their potential. Therefore, you are taking action based upon the findings of your research. Crucially, the actions must also be evaluated as part of the research process and not post-research, as often occurs with the findings from a case study. During action research, many students will amend and evaluate practice multiple times before the research process ends. Thus, those electing to undertake action research usually have a good understanding of the issue at hand, either through personal experience or extensive research on the topic before selecting this approach.

To help you conceptualise the process further, Figure 6.2 highlights the clear procedure that is undertaken in the action research approach. This is adapted from Keegan (2016: 257), who stresses the rigorous pursuit of reflection and action throughout the action research process.

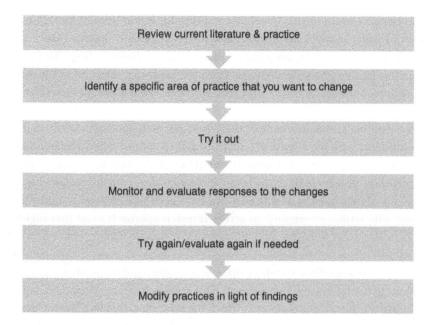

Figure 6.2   Action research procedure

— Action research example —

Paul worked in a special school supporting learners with additional sensory and communication needs. He had noticed that the digital assessment tool that his school used to track learners' progress was not always fit for purpose for every learner. Paul wanted, first, to identify the issues with the current system, exploring the literature on effective assessment of learners with additional sensory and communication needs and, second, to devise and trial a new system for assessing a sampled number of pupils across the school. The action research approach was the most effective for meeting Paul's research aims. This is because he not only wanted to investigate a problem that he had identified but also to take action to change his practice, with the intention that his study would result in pedagogical improvements.

Positives and drawbacks of the action research approach

Action research can be an excellent choice for researchers who are particularly motivated to change an aspect of practice, with the aim of improving both the teaching and pupils' learning experience. It can be a good way of supporting professional development for those working in education as, invariably, a successful action research project results in advances in pedagogical understanding and improvements in practice. Many students in special and inclusive education have links with educational settings. This approach can therefore be a good logistical choice. However, as always, selection of the methodological approach should be driven primarily by the research aims/questions rather than logistical ease.

Both a positive and a drawback of the action research approach are its multi-stage nature. Students who have limited time in which to conduct their research may find that the continual process of reflection and action is difficult to complete. However, this multi-stage process is likely to result in higher-level conclusion drawing, as different layers of data have been gathered and have been reflected upon multiple times. A student who wishes to employ an action research approach must thoroughly plan their timescales, so as to ensure that all stages are completed before the research draws to a close.

It is especially important to reflect upon any professional biases that you may hold when electing to undertake action research. This approach can be particularly vulnerable to professional biases, as the context in which the research takes place is often personally or professionally linked to the researcher. Many students either work in or have other personal links to the educational contexts that they research in; they often come to the research process with an opinion on what should be changed about their pedagogy to result in positive outcomes. Continual reflection upon these opinions is vital, so as to ensure that biases do not cloud the researcher's judgement when gathering data and drawing conclusions.

As explored in the case study approach section, criticisms in relation to generalisability can be levelled towards the action research approach. This is due to the single context that typically characterises the approach.

Checkpoint 6.2

- Action research involves simultaneously gathering data, reflecting upon those data and effecting change, usually in an educational context.
- It involves empirical research – you will therefore gather data in the setting with 'live' participants.
- This approach is worth considering if you have identified a problem that you would like to investigate and attempt to solve during the research process.
- The main difference between case study and action research is that a case study ends when the researcher has investigated an issue of interest while action research continues by attempting to make improvements related to that issue.

Approach 3: Systematic literature review

A systematic literature review is arguably the most common non-empirical methodological approach employed by researchers in special and inclusive education. Its non-empirical nature means that researchers are gathering and analysing secondary data from other authors/sources rather than gathering primary data 'in the field', as with the two methodological approaches previously explored in this chapter. These data can take many forms but will usually include analysing prior research and/or analysing large-scale data sets that have been collected by other researchers. A useful core text in navigating the details associated with the systematic literature review approach is:

Boland, A., Cherry, G. and Dickson, R. (eds) (2017) *Doing a Systematic Review: A Student's Guide.* London: Sage.

In order to conduct a successful systematic literature review, researchers must spend a significant amount of time identifying and setting clear parameters for their sampling of data. If a researcher rushes this step, the whole study can become invalid quite quickly. To ensure validity of your study, you must include all relevant literature that your sampling strategy generates in your data analysis. Therefore, it is vital that your sampling strategy is methodologically sound. Students should consider the following in planning their sampling procedure:

- What are my key words in searching the literature? Will these key words ensure that my search results are relevant?
- Which years of publication am I interested in?
- Which sources am I interested in? A handful of practice-based journals, government publications, large-scale studies, small-scale studies, etc.
- Which search engines will I use?
- What are the geographical parameters of my study? Am I interested in international literature, or only that of the country in which I am studying, for example?
- How will I ensure that the amount of data that my search generates will be manageable?
- How will I identify literature that is irrelevant to my study, and how will I justify its exclusion from my data analysis?

The systematic literature review can be a very good choice for students who are interested in a topic/issue in special and inclusive education on which there is already a good range of published research. It is important that students avoid conducting research that is similar to that already undertaken by others, as this is unlikely to contribute to the body of knowledge in their given field. Therefore, if a student has an interest that has a range of relevant and recent research linked to it then exploring and evaluating that research in greater depth, via a systematic review, can be an excellent approach. This can result in the identification of a range of common themes in the existing literature, which can be invaluable in supporting others plan further empirical research and pedagogical advancements.

In our experience, the field of special and inclusive education can heavily lend itself to small-scale, empirical research studies. This can be for many reasons but is often due to the perceived uniqueness of the contexts in which researchers in this field are interested. Therefore, a range of single case studies and action research projects exist in the literature in relation to many areas of interest in special and inclusive education. Planning a study that attempts to pull these existing studies together and explore commonalities and differences between them could be a very useful contribution to the field. However, be aware that this is not a good choice of methodological approach for a student wishing to explore an issue on which there is very limited published research.

Systematic literature review example

Robert worked as a prison educator, teaching a range of qualifications. Robert was keen to understand more about effective pedagogy in such a specialist environment and was aware that some other prisons had mentoring systems in place to support better engagement in education. These mentoring systems broadly involved one learner supporting a range of other learners with attendance and achievement in the educational courses that the prisons offered. Robert was interested in exploring existing research in the prison education sector to identify any specific pedagogical approaches that resulted in better engagement with education in this context. A systematic literature review was the most appropriate choice for Robert as he was interested in exploring secondary sources of published studies, to inform his own pedagogical decision-making post-study. Rather than implement a mentoring system with little prior evidence as to whether or not it was likely to be successful, Robert chose to use his research time to gain a more evidence-based understanding of effective pedagogy in the sector in which he worked. This study resulted in some very interesting findings, which Robert later used to make changes to his pedagogy.

Positives and drawbacks of the systematic literature review approach

Students often highlight that one of the most positive aspects of the systematic literature review approach links to its non-empirical nature. Students are not required to go 'into the field' to collect data and are therefore not subject to the logistical challenges that can be associated with an empirical approach. Students need not be concerned about withdrawal of participation from people involved in their study and they can manage the timetable of their study without dealing with the unpredictability of educational settings. This can be a particularly helpful factor for students who do not have existing links with educational settings. However, logistics alone should never dictate the methodological approach followed; the main driver of any study should be the research questions and aims.

It is important to highlight a potential ethical drawback of following the systematic review approach. As the approach relies exclusively on data gathered by other researchers, there is no way to ensure that the research analysed was conducted with optimal ethical consideration or, indeed, is valid and reliable. Therefore, it is important to consider whether the authors have identified any ethical tensions or specific considerations in their write-up; if there are any glaring ethical omissions/issues then this should be noted in your study. In general, studies published in peer-reviewed journals tend to be ethically sound; be more wary of literature that is published in other places, such as teaching magazines, newspapers and websites, as they can often read as opinion pieces rather than sound academic studies and can lack rigour. However, when data are sampled effectively, the systematic literature review can have high levels of generalisability to the wider field, as the conclusions drawn are often informed by a large number of studies.

Finally, the systematic literature review approach can quickly sample vast amounts of data that can become unmanageable if not managed effectively. Record keeping is particularly important with this approach; using suitable software can be the difference between a successful and unsuccessful review. Consult the core text by Boland et al. (2017) for more support with this aspect of planning a successful systematic literature review. Remember that all relevant literature that your sampling procedure selects must be analysed in your review; avoid falling into the trap of drawing conclusions/ identifying findings too early on in the process and then only sampling data that reinforces those conclusions. Your aim is to provide the best analysis of the data in your area of interest as possible; this will rarely result in findings common to all of the literature you read.

─ Checkpoint 6.3 ─

- A systematic literature review involves analysing secondary data, previously published by researchers in your area of interest.
- It involves non-empirical research, therefore can be thought of as 'desk based' and will not involve gathering data in the field.
- This approach is worth considering if there is already a significant amount of published research in your area of interest.

Approach 4: Mixed methods

The notion of mixed methods as a methodological approach is somewhat complex and contested in existing literature, particularly in the field of education. Some conceptualise the approach as a methodology involving its own ontology and epistemology, whilst others view it simply as involving more than one method. We have seen the popularity of mixed methods as a methodological approach increase significantly in the field of special and inclusive education over the past few years and so feel it is important to explore some of this confusion with you, so that you are well prepared to plan, execute and write up a mixed methods study, if this is what you choose to do.

For the purposes of this book, we view it as unhelpful to enter the debate on mixed methods as a methodology in any depth. We will simply set out what we mean by mixed methods as a methodological approach; we will do this by giving a basic definition and then highlighting the differences, as we see them, between some confusingly similar terminology related to this approach. We will then move straight into the characteristics of the approach and the positives and drawbacks of it. Don't let the complexity of the concepts associated with this approach put you off from selecting this methodological approach if it is a best fit for your research aims; once we've dealt with the confusing terminology, the process will seem relatively straightforward.

Defining mixed methods

In its simplest terms, the definition by Kumar (2019: 21) is one that we find affinity with, as it translates to the field of special and inclusive education: 'In extremely simple terms, mixed methods is an approach, rather than a philosophy, to social enquiry that uses two or more methods...in undertaking a research study.' These two data-collection methods generally include the gathering and/or analysis of both qualitative and quantitative data. Therefore, data is usually gathered in both word and number form, for example by conducting interviews (word based) and analysing questionnaires (number based).

A note on terminology

To help you in writing up a mixed methods study, it is important to remember that the words 'mixed' and 'methods' can be used in a range of similar combinations but can have very different meanings. We often see students use 'mixed methods' in their write-ups to mean both a methodological approach and the nature of the data-collection methods they have used. It is important to use different terminology to demonstrate an understanding of the differences between these two concepts.

Try to remember these differences, as articulated below, in your writing so that your methodology is written as effectively as possible:

- *Mixed methods methodological approach*: This term should be used when describing the approach you have selected to gather and analyse data in a given study. 'I undertook a mixed methods methodological approach in order to meet the aims of my study...'
- *Methods that are mixed in nature*: This term should be used to highlight that you have used both quantitative and qualitative data-collection methods. You can employ methods that are mixed in nature in a range of methodological approaches, for

example in case study/action research. However, each study should follow only one methodological approach. 'Within my mixed methods methodological approach, I employed methods that were mixed in nature in order to meet the aims of my study...'

The mixed methods approach is usually an example of empirical research, as it almost always involves collecting data from participants in the field, via at least one of the data-collection methods employed. A mixed methods approach is usually employed when a researcher attempts to investigate complex concepts, complex to the extent that 'single methods approaches might result in partial, selective and incomplete understanding' (Cohen et al., 2018: 175).

You may now be thinking that this sounds somewhat similar to both the case study approach and the action research approach in that more than one method is usually employed to collect data within those approaches. The selection of the optimal methodological approach can, therefore, be confusing for those of you who know that employing multiple data-collection methods will be necessary to meeting your research aims. However, the simplest way to decide which approach is best is to think about the context of your research. If you wish to undertake research in a specific context, for example a school/college, then the case study or action research approaches are likely to be a better choice for you than mixed methods. Put simply, mixed methods is a good choice if you have ruled out approaches that are bound by specific contexts.

Mixed methods example

Fiona was studying for an MA in Education, with a focus on special educational needs, disability and inclusion. She was interested in exploring the ways in which primary school teachers in her geographical region who identified themselves as having additional mental health needs navigated their teaching role alongside their mental health needs. The mixed methods approach was the most appropriate for Fiona; the study did not take place in a 'bounded system' as Fiona sampled a large range of teachers in different primary schools in her area. Fiona implemented methods that were mixed in nature in her study; she sent out quantitative surveys to the teachers who gave consent to participate and she undertook qualitative interviews with a small number of the teachers who were happy to share their experiences in greater depth.

Positives and drawbacks of the mixed methods approach

One significant positive of the mixed methods approach is that it can often yield rich and reliable data because both qualitative and quantitative methods are employed in this approach. This results in triangulation of the data, increasing the overall validity of a study. Triangulation is the principle of employing multiple data-collection methods to better support the conclusions drawn through analysing multiple data sources, with the result adding, 'rigor, breadth, complexity, richness, and depth to any inquiry' (Denzin and Lincoln, 2012: 7). However, all methodological approaches explored in this chapter can ensure triangulation as long as multiple data-collection methods are employed, irrespective of whether they are quantitative or qualitative.

Mixed methods is also a very versatile approach in the sense that it can be a good choice in exploring a wide range of topics and areas of interest. The researcher is not confined by the tenets of a particular method of research, as in action research or the case study. The breadth of the approach can allow the researcher to select from a wide range of data-collection methods; this can often support collection of most relevant data and ensure that the methods selected are the best fit for meeting the research aims.

However, this breadth and flexibility could also be seen as a drawback. Without careful planning, a mixed methods approach can become too broad and lack specificity in conclusion drawing. Another potential weakness relates to epistemology and is explored in the next section.

Checkpoint 6.4

- The mixed methods approach is a good choice for students whose research interest is not bounded by specific contexts (for example, schools/colleges).
- In its simplest form, the mixed methods approach involves collection of data by employing two or more methods. These are usually a combination of quantitative and qualitative.
- Ensure that you are confident with the terminology you use in your write-up of this approach; spend time identifying the difference between the 'mixed methods approach' and 'data-collection methods that are mixed in nature'.

A note on epistemology and the methodological approach

At this point, it is helpful to reflect back to where we started on this journey to conducting a successful research project, with the 'ologies' we explored in Chapter 2. The two camps of researcher position that we explored in this chapter are important in determining which methodological approaches are most appropriate for you to consider as an individual researcher. To recap, 'positivist' researchers believe that knowledge exists independently of perception. Therefore, positivist researchers will be unlikely to select methodological approaches that involve collecting perception-based data from individuals. Consequently, it is unlikely that positivist researchers will elect to follow either case study or action research approaches.

Conversely, post-positivist researchers believe that knowledge is subjective and context dependent; the case study and/or action research methodological approaches are therefore likely to appeal to researchers that follow this epistemological view-point. It may be helpful for you to revisit the answers you gave to the activity in Chapter 2 to ensure that your ontological and epistemological views align with the methodological approaches you are most interested in, having explored those pre-sented in this chapter.

There is a notable tension between epistemology and the mixed methods method-ological approach. Some have argued that quantitative and qualitative data-collection methods should not be undertaken together, as they hinder a researcher from strictly taking account of their epistemological views, since you cannot be in both camps of researcher position. Others have taken a more relaxed approach to this, some terming the mixed methods approach as a 'third camp'. This third camp was explored in Chapter 2. The crucial question to ask yourself is whether or not you feel that, 'the methodology of the physical sciences can be applied to the study of social phenomena' (Kumar, 2019: 33). If you believe that it cannot then it is helpful for you to read more about research approaches that employ purely quantitative data-collection methods, for example quasi-experimental research.

Selecting the most appropriate methodological approach

To help you in selecting the most appropriate methodological approach from those we have explored in this chapter, we have devised a simple flow chart (see Figure 6.3). This flow chart encourages you to answer questions that will direct you to an appro-priate approach for further exploration. It should be noted that this chart does not include all possible methodological approaches for you to select from, simply those that are most common in this field and have been explored in this chapter. Additional approaches will be explored in Chapter 9. A range of factors over and above those presented in the chart should be explored when selecting your approach so all potential choices should be discussed with your supervisor before you commit to an approach.

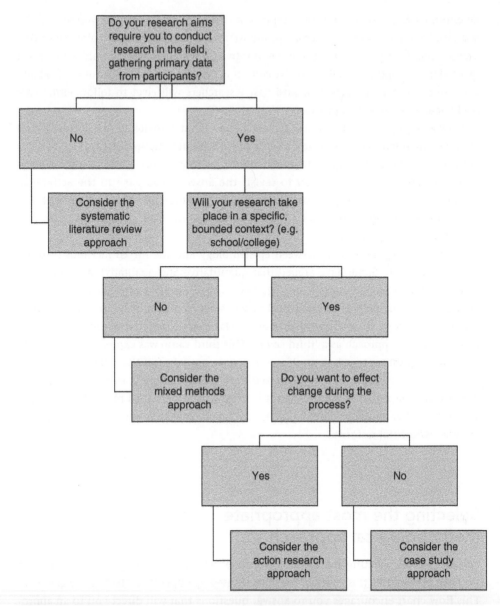

Figure 6.3 Choosing an appropriate methodological approach

Which methodological approach?

Read the research interests of the students in Table 6.1 below and try to identify which methodological approach(es) could be a good fit for investigating them. The answers are at the end of the chapter.

Table 6.1 Matching research interests and methodological approaches

Research interests
1   I am an MA Education student, working in higher education, and am interested in exploring ways in which materials and resources could be more effectively adapted for the students I teach who have dyslexia. After analysing some approaches, I want to trial an approach to determine whether or not my students find it beneficial.
2   I work in a primary school and have noticed that some children identified with ASD often find lunchtimes difficult. I want to explore the reasons why this might be the case in my school.
3   As well as studying, I volunteer for an organisation supporting young people who identify themselves as LGBT. I have noticed that many of the young people I work with have lower than average school attendance. I want to explore prior studies that have researched low school attendance and those that have implemented programmes/strategies to improve young people's attendance. I hope to use any potentially successful strategies to inform my volunteer work after my studies have ended.
4   I am a headteacher of a small special school. Our school struggles with parental engagement. I would like to use my research time to explore parental engagement strategies across a range of special schools in my region, primarily by surveying other special school headteachers, but also by conducting interviews with some parents of children in special schools across my local area.

Chapter summary

This chapter has highlighted four of the most common methodological approaches in special and inclusive education. We have explored the key features of each of these approaches and highlighted a range of positives and potential drawbacks of each approach. We have also highlighted some acknowledged tensions in existing literature around the definitions of and terminology used in describing these four approaches, with particular reference to mixed methods. To close this chapter, it may be helpful for you to reflect upon the following bullet points, so that you are ready to move further on in this book and explore some common data-collection methods used in the field of special and inclusive education.

- Your research question, aims and objectives will always be the main driver in determining which methodological approach to employ.
- Your choice of research design will be largely influenced by whether you view yourself as a positivist or post-positivist and, therefore, whether you choose to undertake an empirical or non-empirical approach to data collection.
- You should ensure that you are aware of both the positives and drawbacks of each approach you are considering before you make your final selection. Identifying the drawbacks will strengthen your data collection and analysis as well as your write-up.
- Follow your interests; research is often a deeply personal journey. Ensure that you are comfortable with and motivated by your choice of methodological approach before you plan further.

Recommended reading

The recommended reading for this chapter is embedded within the exploration of each of the methodological approaches. Please refer back to these sections to identify the core text that we recommend you consult to broaden your knowledge of each specific approach.

Activity 6.1 answers

1. Action research. 2. Case study (unless the student wishes to change practice during the research process, in which case action research would be appropriate). 3. Systematic literature review. 4. Mixed methods or multiple case study. (This will depend on the number of contexts that this student is interested in researching. If they wish to conduct in-depth research in three or four schools, a multiple case study would be appropriate. If they wish to survey other headteachers/speak to parents of children from a large number of special schools, mixed methods is most appropriate.)

7

LISTENING: COLLECTING DATA USING INTERVIEWS AND QUESTIONNAIRES

━━━━━━━ **Chapter objectives** ━━━━━━━

By the end of this chapter you will:

✓ Recognise a range of interview and questionnaire types
✓ Have reflected on the relative strengths and limitations of different types of interviews and questionnaires
✓ Understand the difference between open and closed questions and when each should be used
✓ Be able to identify the range of factors that need to be considered in conducting an effective interview and designing an effective questionnaire
✓ Have considered how to adapt interviews and questionnaires to take account of the abilities and communication preferences of those for whom it is designed

Introduction

The next three chapters focus on the data-gathering stage of the research process. Together, they will help you decide which data-collection methods will be most suitable for your particular research questions. This first chapter introduces two of the most widely used data-gathering methods: interviews and questionnaires. Both involve learning about people's knowledge, views and experiences by asking questions and both can be designed and deployed flexibly. This makes them suitable for a wide range of research purposes and approaches.

In this chapter we briefly introduce a range of interview and questionnaire approaches before focusing more closely on some of the issues that need to be considered when using these methods. We then move to how these methods might be adapted if your project involves working with participants with SEND. As this book is aimed primarily at research students and practitioner researchers, the content, examples and case studies reflect our assumption that most readers will be engaging in small-scale qualitative studies.

Interviews and questionnaires: An overview

Research texts frequently distinguish between different interview approaches according to the degree to which they are structured. At one end of the continuum is the **structured interview**. This refers to interview situations where each participant is asked the same set of questions in the same order. They suit situations where the researcher needs short, specific answers rather than ones that require greater depth, detail or explanation. They are often used in quantitative research where the short-answer format allows statistical analysis.

At the other end of the continuum are **unstructured interviews**. Buckler and Walliman (2016) describe these as a free-flowing exchange between the interviewer and the interviewee. There are no set questions and the interviewer has much less input into the direction and focus of the interview. This approach is particularly suitable for ethnographic approaches 'where the researcher does not have preconceived ideas about what they expect to find' (Burton et al., 2014: 134).

Lying between these two approaches is the **semi-structured interview**. Here, the interview is guided by a set of key questions that are presented to each participant but additional questions may also be asked – for instance, questions that seek further clarification or detail. This means that the exact number, type and order of questions will vary between participants. This approach allows the interviewer to go off in different directions to seek greater depth in relation to some questions if the interviewee is particularly knowledgeable in that area. Semi-structured interviews are frequently used in qualitative research.

We also draw attention to **focus group interviews**. This refers to situations where participants are interviewed as part of a group, normally ranging between five and ten members. This approach is suitable for situations where the researcher wants participants to share or discuss experiences and perspectives. We don't provide additional detail in this chapter (although we direct you to a good source in our Recommended reading) but we mention it here as a reminder that interviews do not have to be a one-to-one encounter. If your participants are children, the one-to-one interview situation may be unfamiliar and therefore intimidating. Pairs and small groups (three or four members), on the other hand, may provide the comfort and security that enable children to share their thoughts and experiences. They also support data richness due to the way in which participants often build upon others' contributions to the discussion.

Questionnaires can be thought of as written interviews where each respondent is presented with the same questions in the same format and order. In this respect, they resemble a structured interview. However, like interviews, they can also vary greatly in the degree of structure. Highly structured questionnaires consist entirely of closed, short-answer questions that lend themselves to quantitative analysis. Semi-structured questionnaires might also include open questions with spaces or comment boxes that allow participants to write their responses in their own words. This makes them more suitable for qualitative studies that aim to collect more descriptive and explanatory detail. The latter take longer to collate and analyse and this needs to be taken into account when determining your sample size. In general, the larger the sample, the more structured a questionnaire needs to be.

Both questionnaires and interviews offer a range of strengths and limitations that should be considered when deciding which method is suitable for your particular research. Table 7.1 summarises some of these.

Table 7.1 Strengths and limitations of semi-structured approaches

Semi-structured interviews	
Strengths	*Limitations*
• Provide large amounts of rich, detailed data (useful if you want in-depth understandings and insights)	• Time consuming (participants need to be recruited and dates, times and venues agreed; transcription is time consuming)
• Allow a dialogue (you can follow up with a related question to gain greater detail and depth of understanding)	• Possible interviewer effects (the face-to-face nature of an interview and the presence of recording equipment may inhibit honest and free expression)
• May result in unexpected useful information	• Analysis and interpretation are more complex than with a more structured questionnaire

(Continued)

Table 7.1 (Continued)

Questionnaires	
Strengths	*Limitations*
• Offer a convenient and efficient way of gaining information from a large number of people (respondents can choose the time and place and take as much or as little time as they want)	• Possibility of low response rate (this threatens the validity of the research)
	• Respondents might interpret a question differently from how you intended (this threatens the validity of the research)
• Allow for anonymity (this eliminates interviewer effects and encourages honesty)	• No opportunity to seek clarification or ask follow-up questions (therefore not suitable if the researcher wants rich, detailed information or in-depth understanding)
• Less demanding of participants (short-answer questions generally require less time and thought than open-ended interview questions)	• Missing data (some respondents may skip some questions)
• The short-answer format that characterises questionnaires means that data is more easily quantified and analysed (particularly relevant to quantitative studies)	• Number and type of questions that can be asked is limited (to eliminate respondent fatigue, a good questionnaire will be limited to about two sides of A4)
	• Not appropriate for participants with low levels of literacy or who are not proficient in English

Please note that no method is inherently better than another. Rather, one method is better than another in a particular context and in relation to particular research aims and objectives. Table 7.1 indicates that qualitative interviews are generally suitable for situations where the researcher wants rich, detailed information and the number of participants is relatively small; questionnaires are good for situations where there is a large number of participants, where anonymity might be important and where the researcher wants specific information that can be gathered through short-answer questions.

Both interviews and questionnaires can be used in a mixed methods approach. In Chapter 3 you met Moana, a teacher and master's student who was interested in learning about other teachers' views and experiences of pupils with fetal alcohol syndrome disorder (FASD). She started with a questionnaire which she distributed online via a teaching network to which she belonged. Although the sort of data she could collect using this method was limited to that which could easily be gathered using short-answer questions, it enabled her to access a large population and get a feel for some commonalities and trends. She then followed up with a small number of in-depth qualitative interviews, which provided detailed, rich accounts that complemented the more superficial data provided by the questionnaires.

Note that methodological choices are not necessarily clear-cut. Although we have presented interviews and questionnaires as two separate methods, both can be deployed flexibly to suit particular research situations. For example, some of our students have created questionnaires to use with children and young people with SEND but they were used in a face-to-face interview-type situation. In these cases, the questionnaire served primarily as a visual aide that supported the interview process.

Checkpoint 7.1

- Interviews and questionnaires are two of the most widely used data-collection methods in special and inclusive education.
- Each offers different strengths and limitations.
- Both can be structured, semi-structured or unstructured.
- Their design can be easily adapted to make them suitable for a wide range of research purposes and approaches.

Issues to consider when preparing your interview or questionnaire

The questions: The 'What?', the 'How?' and the 'How many?'

As is the case with all parts of the research process, successful outcomes require careful planning. One aspect of planning common to both interviews and questionnaires is deciding on the set of questions to ask. We suggest that you start by asking yourself, 'What information do I need in order to answer my research question?' and 'What questions do I therefore need to ask?' Compose a list of all of the possible questions that will help provide that information and then identify which ones overlap and which ones are not needed. Discard those that are not directly relevant to your research question. This will leave you with a smaller, more manageable pool of key questions.

The number of questions is important. It will be a balancing act between asking enough questions to get the information you want, but not so many that you place unrealistic demands on your participants. Aim to keep your questionnaire or interview as short as possible for the information you need. People are more likely to agree to a 40-minute interview than an 80-minute one, and questionnaire respondents are more likely to complete a short questionnaire than a long one. We like Buckler and Walliman's advice about questionnaires and share it with our students. 'The golden rule when preparing a questionnaire is to KISS it: Keep It Short and Simple' (2016: 200). We recommend keeping your questionnaire to the equivalent of about two sides of A4.

Whether it be an interview or a questionnaire, the order in which the questions are presented may also affect how participants respond. Starting with simple, non-contentious questions that don't require a lot of thought is a good way of easing participants into the process and helps them feel that they are progressing (Burton et al., 2014).

How you phrase your questions also requires consideration. Closed questions are those that can be answered in just a few words, or with a simple yes or no, or involve selecting an answer from a fixed number of alternatives such as those offered in multi-choice questions. They are typically used in questionnaires and are good for gaining straightforward, factual information. Open questions invite an extended answer and are typically used in qualitative interviews. They seek rich detail, explanations and examples. Sometimes an open question may not be phrased as a question but rather as an invitation to share thoughts and experiences – for instance, 'Tell me about a time when you...'. Similarly, it might be phrased as a closed question that suggests a yes or no answer, but is interpreted as a prompt to add more detail – for instance, 'Can you share a specific example of that?'. Many qualitative interviews and questionnaires use a mix of both but the balance of open to closed questions should be weighted more heavily towards the former. When researching with children and young people, consider adding some context that will help them answer the question. For example, rather than simply asking, 'How would you describe your school?', you could ask, 'If you were talking to another child who was thinking about coming to your school, what would you tell them about it?'.

It's also important not to assume that people will interpret a question in the way you intended. Particularly with questionnaires, avoiding ambiguity is surprisingly difficult. In interviews, a participant's response will often make it obvious when a question has been misunderstood but the dialogic nature of an interview allows you to rephrase your question or to clarify what you are asking. However, this is not the case for questionnaires. This makes piloting especially important. At the very least, always seek feedback from others about the wording, order, clarity of questions (and in the case of questionnaires, the formatting) as this will support better research outcomes. We share some common pitfalls and how to avoid them shortly.

Issues that apply specifically to interviews

Interviews often involve direct face-to-face contact with participants. This results in a number of additional issues that are not applicable to questionnaires. Each has the potential to enhance or inhibit both the quantity and quality of data you collect.

Activity 7.1

Consider your interview process

A school has agreed that you can undertake one-to-one interviews with staff on your chosen topic. Formal consent has been gained and interview times arranged. Before reading on, consider your answers to the questions below.

1   How will you establish rapport and put participants at ease?

2   How will you record participants' answers to your questions?
3   What range of communication skills will be important for a successful interview?
4   What question starters might be good for gaining additional depth?

The 'when'

The key question here is how to minimise any possible disruption or inconvenience to the interviewee? Much educational research is only made possible because of the goodwill of school staff, parents and students who willingly give their time to participate in research, often for little or no direct reward. It is therefore important to minimise cost and inconvenience. For example, in one study, interviews with learning support assistants took place during their normal work day while the SENCO covered for them. This avoided having to use their lunch break or interviewing them after school when they had other commitments. This, of course, is not always possible but the point to bear in mind is to be flexible with regard to when, where and how interviews take place, and to give participants as much choice and control as possible. For example, if participants prefer a phone, Zoom or email interview, then aim to accommodate their wishes.

The 'where'

The physical setting is another factor to consider. Think about the extent to which your interview space will help create the relaxed, informal atmosphere that will support open and honest dialogue. Consider, for example, if background noise will be a problem, whether someone might prefer to be interviewed on site (for convenience) or off site (for greater privacy). Are you and your interviewee seated at the same physical level, and with no barriers (such as a desk) between you? Sitting at a right angle allows easy eye contact but also means that interviewer and interviewee are not constantly staring at each other. Is the seating comfortable? What about room temperature and light? There will inevitably be compromises, not least because you may have little control over where your interview takes place. Sometimes your interviewee will decide, and in a school setting there may be little choice. Nevertheless, where possible, aim to find or create an interview space that will work well for your interviewee.

The interview process

Ann Oakley's (1981) widely cited article on qualitative interviewing emphasises that first and foremost an interview is a relational encounter. This means that good research outcomes require trust and respect. There is no single best way to undertake an interview but thinking through how you might connect well with your interviewee and convey your interest and appreciation will help get you off to a good start. Plan how you will greet your participants. What will you say first to help put them at ease? How will you convey appreciation for their time and that you value their perspectives? Share a little about yourself and check that they understand the purpose of the interview. Emphasise that there are no right or wrong answers and remind them of their ethical rights.

Once the interview starts, use active listening skills such as minimal encouragers (short utterances such as 'yes' or 'ah-ha') and paraphrasing (a short summary of what has just been said). The former conveys that you are listening carefully while the latter provides an opportunity for participants to confirm or correct your interpretation of something they said. Adopt a non-judgemental stance to whatever is said. This helps convey respect and encourage honesty. Think about your body language as well. Is it open? Consider eye contact; you want some but not too much. Gestures such as nodding your head indicate understanding. Remember that open questions are likely to require some thought on the part of the participants so it's important to be comfortable with silent pauses and to allow enough time for thinking and responding. Use prompts to encourage further elaboration. Questions such as, 'Can you tell me a little more about that?' or 'Can you give me an example of that?' may yield some useful additional detail. Practise with friends or classmates before your first interview and seek feedback from them about your questions and interview style. Consider making your last question, 'What haven't I asked that you think I should have?' or 'What would you like to tell me that I haven't asked you about?' There may be something important that you simply hadn't thought about.

To record or not to record?

It's a good idea to record your interviews. There are several reasons for this. First, you won't remember everything that participants say and therefore may miss important points – but taking copious notes during the interview might be distracting to them. Recording interviews allows you to focus fully on what your interviewee is saying and leaves you better placed to clarify meaning or seek additional detail. Audio recording is simple and unobtrusive. Small digital audio recorders are inexpensive and most phones have a recording function that allow you to download files onto a computer for storage and transcription. Video recording takes longer to transcribe but captures body language as well as words, so may be particularly appropriate for some research. Either way, if you are working with children allow time for them to become familiar with the presence of your recording device. Don't forget to check and test the equipment and to consider if the venue is quiet enough to allow a good recording. One student undertook her first interview in a coffee shop. While this afforded both her and her parent participant a neutral and informal space (and allowed her to buy her participant a coffee), she subsequently found this interview very difficult to transcribe because of the background noise.

Transcribing

Interview recordings are usually transcribed. One of the first things you will notice when doing this is that a verbal account is quite different from a written one. People don't talk in grammatically correct sentences, or even in identifiable sentences! There will be pauses, ums and ahhs, repetitions and possibly short inaudible sections where you are not actually sure what was said. You will need to make a decision about what level of detail is required for your particular research. Do you need a full transcription that includes details about paralanguage (non-verbal elements such as pauses, tone, speed, laughter) or will a partial transcription that summarises the less relevant parts of the interview but provides a word-for-word account of other parts suffice? Either way, be sure to allow plenty of time for transcribing. Different research texts suggest slightly different times but most agree that transcription time can take up to four times the length of the interview. Transcription software is available but can be expensive. The 'voice memo' tool available in Google Docs may be a useful way of supporting transcription and is free to use for those with a Gmail account.

Activity 7.2

Different approaches to interviewing

Interviews can be conducted in many different ways – for example, face-to-face, telephone, synchronous online via a chat app, asynchronous via email or using a video platform such as Zoom or Teams. There is no single best approach. You will need to assess the relative strengths and limitations of any given method in order to identify what will produce good results for your particular research. Focusing just on the first three approaches noted above, identify two possible advantages and limitations for each. You will find some of our ideas at the end of the chapter.

Issues that apply specifically to questionnaires

Constructing a good questionnaire may appear to be a simple and straightforward task. In reality, this is far from the case. First, there is a wide range of possible question formats from which to choose. The combination of question types that will work best for your particular project will be determined by the sorts of information you need.

Four common short-answer formats are:

- Dichotomous questions: Respondents select one of two possible alternatives
- Multiple-choice questions: Respondents select from three or more alternatives
- Rank ordering questions: Respondents rank items according to perceived importance
- Rating scales: Respondents indicate where they would place themselves on the scale provided

As the degree of detail we can provide in this chapter is limited, we strongly urge you to access the chapter by Cohen et al. (2018) listed in Recommended reading at the end of this chapter. It provides a comprehensive overview of question types typically used in questionnaires and also some of the pitfalls. Below, we illustrate five pitfalls commonly experienced by our students and how they might be avoided.

1   Long, complex questions

Questions that are too long, or require several readings to make sense of, are likely to be left blank by respondents who want to move through the questionnaire quickly.

2   Questions that are ambiguous or open to interpretation

Example: How often do you meet with your mentor?

☐ Very often   ☐ Often   ☐ Not very often   ☐ Never

In this example, 'often' is open to interpretation. Instead, it would be better to make the options more specific, such as:

More than once a week   About once a week   Less than once a week   Never

3   Asking more than one thing within a single question (sometimes referred to as a double question).

Example: How satisfied were you with the support your child received from the teacher and the teaching assistant?

Very satisfied   Mostly satisfied   Somewhat satisfied   Not satisfied

Respondents may not be sure how to answer this if they were very satisfied with the support their child received from the teaching assistant but only somewhat satisfied with the support received from the teacher. It would be better to break this into two separate questions.

4   Presenting respondents with alternatives that are not mutually exclusive.

Example: How many years have you worked as a SENCO in this setting?

1–5   5–10   10–15   More than 15

If the respondent has worked as a SENCO for five years, it is unclear which box they should tick. Instead, the options should be mutually exclusive (for example: 1–5; 6–10; 11–15; more than 15).

5   Offering options that do not allow for the full range of possible answers.

Example: Does your child attend their IEP (individual education plan) meetings?

Yes   No

A respondent will not know how to answer this question if the child attends some meetings but not others. Adding 'sometimes' as an option would improve this question.

As noted earlier for interviews, it is important to think through the logistics so that cost and inconvenience for respondents is minimised. This will improve your response rate. Additionally, be sure to include clear instructions on what respondents should do with the questionnaire once it is completed. For example, one student left a postbox construction at the school office and the questionnaire explained that it would be collected at the end of the week. This gave respondents four days in which to complete the questionnaire as well as a simple way of returning the questionnaire to the researcher which also provided anonymity. Another student included an addressed, pre-paid envelope with her questionnaire, thus enabling respondents to complete it where and when it was convenient. Online questionnaires avoid logistics such as these but rely on respondents accessing a device and engaging with the questionnaire.

Finally, check that the formatting is professional and clear. This includes ensuring that the questionnaire is visually appealing, doesn't look cluttered, uses an appropriate font size for the audience, and is easy to read and follow. Always seek feedback from others before using your questionnaire.

Adapting methods

If your study involves the direct participation of those with SEND, you will need to adapt how you conduct your interview or design your questionnaire to accommodate different developmental levels and communication preferences. Ethical research also requires that you think about how to reduce the power differential between the researcher and the participant. This is an important element of respecting and valuing what participants can share. Below, we offer some suggestions and illustrate with some examples.

First, think about how you can make the research setting as informal, relaxing and enjoyable as possible. For example, use a setting that participants are familiar with and feel comfortable in. For interviews, consider a 'walking tour' rather than a sit-down interview, or incorporate arts and play-based activities with which children are already familiar (see Chapter 9).

Multisensory approaches are great for supporting inclusivity. Visual scaffolds and concrete materials help accommodate the lower linguistic or literacy skills of some participants. A questionnaire that uses simple language and where text is supported by pictures and diagrams is helpful for a pupil who has moderate learning difficulties, but equally helpful for a pupil with dyslexia, ASD or one whose first language is not English. The spoken questions in an interview are transitory and therefore have to be remembered whereas visual stimuli and concrete materials are tangible and enduring. They also provide a focus and reduce the need for eye contact, which might be stressful for some participants. Additionally, tablets and other devices are increasingly used in educational contexts. They provide popular and engaging tools for learners and also offer possibilities for adapting research methods. Mayne et al. (2017), for example, used a touchscreen and 'assent' and 'dissent' faces to enable the two three-year-olds in their study to indicate their willingness to start and continue in the research process.

Providing options is another way of increasing comfort and accessibility. In interview situations, for example, some participants might prefer to be interviewed with a friend, a classmate or in a small group rather than one to one. Some might prefer to be interviewed by a trusted adult than by someone they do not know. As noted earlier, today's technology opens up a range of distance interview possibilities, thus avoiding the possible discomfort of meeting with a stranger. Similarly, if your research requires participants to keep some sort of diary or journal, there are multiple ways of doing this. For higher functioning individuals, it could be a traditional written diary, and for others, it could be a template that the researcher has prepared in advance, or for others, an audio or video diary.

Next, aim to tailor the approach to the individuals concerned as much as possible. This requires familiarising time in the setting and also seeking guidance from others about participants' abilities and communication preferences. It also requires a flexible design that, where possible, offers participants choice and control over how to engage with the research. While this places extra demands on the researcher, it also opens up research possibilities to those whose voices are all too often neglected in research.

Example 1

In her research on the educational self-perceptions of children with Down's syndrome, Begley (2000) used a range of visual and concrete materials to help accommodate the oral language and comprehension difficulties typically experienced by learners with Down's syndrome. The study took place across a range of special and mainstream settings with children of varying ages and abilities. She makes the point that different data-collection methods will work better for different children and that this requires familiarisation time. An example of a method she used with one group of children was postboxes affixed with clock faces with graduated shading that indicated three possible responses to her questions: all, some or none of the time. She trialled it in a pilot study and found this to be the preferred and easiest to understand method for those particular children. It overcame their verbal communication difficulties and provided a concrete focus that helped sustain their attention. Additionally, for children whose receptive or expressive language skills were more severely affected, she sought the help of the teaching assistant who was able to communicate her questions using sign language. This ensured that those learners were not excluded from her research.

Example 2

MacLeod at al. (2014) undertook a small-scale qualitative study with ten higher education students diagnosed with ASD. They wanted to find out how these high-functioning individuals made sense of their educational achievements. The researchers chose semi-structured interviews as their main data-collection method and made several adaptations to create an affirming research process. First, they recognised that although participants all identified as having ASD, their strengths and preferences were likely to be very different. To accommodate this, they offered three different interview options: face to face, telephone, or synchronous (real time) online. As the authors note: 'In offering different participation options, it was hoped that individuals would feel able to contribute in the manner best for them' (MacLeod et al., 2014: 411). They also sent participants the key questions ahead of the interview. This was a way of providing predictability and thus reducing the anxiety that might be felt in a new and unfamiliar situation. Additionally, they set no timeframe on the interview, instead allowing participants to control how much to contribute and how much time was required. This resulted in the interviews ranging from 47 minutes to six hours in duration! The participants were also actively involved in the data-analysis process by being given opportunities to add to or amend their contributions and the researcher's interpretation of these, either on paper or through a second interview process. This helped address the power differential between the researcher and the participants.

Case study 7.1

Nadia, an undergraduate student in education studies, was interested in learning more about the experiences of parents and children with SEND in relation to the support systems available to them. Part of her Year 3 project involved interviewing adolescents with a range of communication difficulties, all of whom had been diagnosed with ASD and had education, health and care (EHC) plans. In preparation, Nadia sought information from the young people's parents and caregivers about how best to explain the project and seek consent from them. Additionally, she asked about their communication preferences and special interests. She used this information to develop a personalised questionnaire that was then used in a face-to-face interview-type situation. It was designed to be accessible (easy to read and follow), attractive (included both text and pictures), and took account of the individual needs and interests of each young person (each questionnaire had some questions specifically related to the young person's particular interests). Additionally, as part of the consent-seeking process, participants could indicate if they preferred to be interviewed at home or at school, and if they wanted to be interviewed by the researcher, by their parent or by the researcher in the presence of a parent. This afforded them more control in the research process. All of the young people chose to complete the questionnaire in the home setting, some face to face with the researcher and some with the assistance of a parent without the researcher being present. Tailoring the research experience in these relatively simple ways provided greater comfort and encouraged the participation of an otherwise hard-to-reach group.

Visual supports

Whether it be an interview where a visual prop is provided or a questionnaire into which a visual scaffold is integrated, visual supports are a useful way of supporting the research process. They provide a focus, help maintain engagement and prompt further discussion. They are easily designed for specific research situations, and we encourage you to create your own. The examples below illustrate.

Example 1

Tamati adapted the template shown in Figure 7.1 as part of his interview research into children's experiences of attending IEP meetings. The question in this instance was: 'How did I feel after attending the IEP meeting?' One child indicated '5', which created opportunities for follow-up questions such as: 'What would need to be different for you to move closer to the smiley face?' The child then recounted that sitting with a group of adults, some of whom he did not know, was hard. He also suggested that knowing what he would be asked beforehand would be better because it would give him more thinking time.

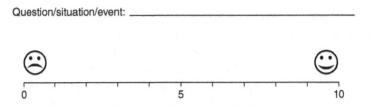

Figure 7.1   Visual aid Example 1

Example 2

Figure 7.2 was used as a visual aid when interviewing children about their experiences using a computer-assisted reading intervention. Used alongside the spoken word, it served as a memory aid for the question being asked, provided a source of focus, and allowed the children to respond either verbally or physically. The graduated question structure meant that rather than responding with either yes or no, participants could indicate degrees of enjoyment. Worthy of note in this example is that the interviews were undertaken by two Year 6 pupils (ten-year-olds) who had been trained for this purpose. This was to reduce the possibility that the children being interviewed would give the answers they thought adults wanted to hear. Importantly, this approached aligned well with other events taking place in school at the time that were also being 'reported on' by pupils.

Did you enjoy using Nessy?

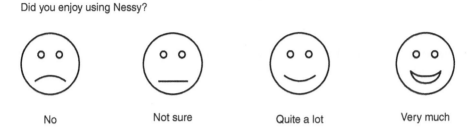

| No | Not sure | Quite a lot | Very much |

Figure 7.2   Visual aid Example 2

Example 3

The visual scaffold shown in Figure 7.3 was used in a doctoral study of an educationally vulnerable group – pregnant schoolgirls and schoolgirl mothers. It aimed to make the interview process more comfortable by giving participants something concrete to focus on and by prompting them to identify different elements of their experience of learning that they were pregnant. It was useful given the very personal nature of some of the interview questions. It shows how one participant responded.

Figure 7.3   Visual aid Example 3

Example 4

Figure 7.4 was used as a visual cue in interviews with young people who had been excluded from school and were attending an alternative educational setting. It aimed to get them thinking holistically about their current setting – the positives, the negatives and also the points of interest.

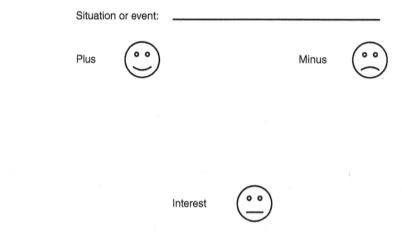

Figure 7.4   Visual aid Example 4

Chapter summary

Interviews and questionnaires are two of the most commonly used data-collection methods in the social sciences. Both can take a range of forms depending on the degree of structure, and both can be deployed face to face or at a distance. This makes them incredibly versatile research tools. Exactly how they are designed and deployed should be guided by your research question and with due consideration given to the relative advantages and disadvantages inherent in any particular approach. Successful use of these tools also requires an approach that minimises some of the pitfalls we have highlighted and takes into consideration the range of issues that could impact the amount and quality of data you gather. Particularly when researching with those with SEND, remember to tailor the approach to the individual as much as possible. This requires some familiarising time in the setting and seeking guidance from those who know participants well. It also requires a flexible design that, where possible, offers participants choice and control over how to engage with the research. Finally, we have made a case for the value of adopting a multisensory approach, and in particular, the use of visual scaffolds. This supports a more inclusive research experience and helps researchers to access the views and experiences of those that are all too frequently neglected in more traditional research.

Table 7.2 Our thoughts on Activity: Different approaches to interviewing

	Advantages	Limitations
Face to face	Establishing connection and building rapport may be easier	Will require arranging a physical space to meet
	Access to body language and paralanguage	There will be time and travel costs
	Easy to incorporate visual scaffolds and activities	Not everyone will be comfortable meeting an unfamiliar adult
Telephone	Able to interview people at a distance (no travel costs)	No access to body language (thus difficult to judge if someone is feeling uncomfortable)
	Less anxiety-producing for those who are uncomfortable meeting strangers	No control over environmental factors for interviewee (e.g. background noise or other distractions)
Computer-mediated (live 'chat' or email)	Able to interview people at a distance	No access to body language and paralanguage
	Less anxiety-producing for those who are uncomfortable meeting strangers	Not suitable for those with limited literacy and typing skills
	Produces a textual record, thus eliminates the need for transcription	Demands of reading and writing mean slower and more tiring interview process
		Requires a good internet connection

Recommended reading

- Barbour, R. (2018) *Doing Focus Groups*, 2nd edn. London: Sage.

Outline: This book provides a comprehensive guide to planning and undertaking successful focus groups. The author explains the relative merits and challenges of group discussions and shares practical ideas for collecting and analysing data.

- Brinkmann, S., Kvale, S. and Flick, U. (2018) *Doing Interviews*, 2nd edn. London: Sage.

Outline: This book provides a concise introduction to the range and scope of interviewing in the social sciences. We particularly recommend Chapter 8 on transcribing interviews as it provides useful additional detail and illustrative examples that have not been included in our chapter.

- Chapter 24 in Cohen, L., Manion, L. and Morrison, K. (2018) *Research Methods in Education*, 8th edn. London: Routledge.

Outline: This easy-to-read chapter provides a detailed guide to designing, piloting and distributing a questionnaire. It provides examples of a range of question types, draws attention to common pitfalls in question writing, and provides useful information on sequencing questions, the layout of the questionnaire and how to process questionnaire data.

- Gripton, C. and Vincent, K. (2021) Using small world toys for research: A method for gaining insight into children's lived experiences of school. *International Journal of Research and Method in Education*, 44(3): 225–40.

Outline: This article illustrates the potential of small world toys as a way of facilitating research conversations with children and thereby tapping into important insights that might otherwise be missed using more traditional methods.

- Pimlott-Wilson, H. (2012) Visualising children's participation in research: Lego Duplo, rainbows and clouds and moodboards. *International Journal of Social Research Methodology*, 15(2): 135–48.

Overview: This article provides a detailed descriptive account of how the researcher used Lego Duplo, 'rainbows and clouds' and moodboards to collect data for her research. She illustrates each with an example of the creative artefacts that children produced. She also discusses the relative strengths and limitations of each method and explains how her understanding of ethical research was applied. This article would be particularly useful for anyone considering using these, or some other form of creative data-collection method.

8

LOOKING: COLLECTING DATA USING OBSERVATION

━━━━━━━━━━━━━ Chapter objectives ━━━━━━━━━━━━━

By the end of this chapter you will:

- ✓ Understand what observation is and what it offers educational research
- ✓ Know how to undertake some different types of observations
- ✓ Have reflected on the range of roles that can be adopted by a researcher in observational studies
- ✓ Be aware of the range of factors that need to be considered when planning an observational study

Introduction

In this second of three chapters on data-collection methods, we turn to observation: the acts of looking and listening. As noted in Chapter 1, it is the systematic approach, adopted for a specific purpose, that differentiates observational research from the more general 'noticing things' that we all engage in every day. In this chapter we look at why observation is important and explore what it can contribute to the research process. We delve briefly into how it has been used historically in educational research before looking at different ways of observing and the range of issues that need to be considered when planning your observational study.

Observation: Past and present

The systematic observation of children for research purposes goes back to the eighteenth century (Mukherji and Albon, 2015). Since then, observation has been widely used by educationalists and psychologists to gain understandings about children's learning, behaviour and development. Many of you will be familiar with the works of Bruner, Erikson, Montessori, Piaget and Vygotsky, all of whom used observation as the basis of their educational theories. Similarly, Bowlby's work on attachment, and its subsequent development by Ainsworth, relied heavily on observation.

Today, observation is used for a wide range of purposes in educational settings. Schools and early childhood settings frequently use observation as a standard record-keeping tool and as part of the formative and summative assessment of learners. It is also used within teacher and teacher trainee appraisal systems (Wragg, 2012) and by practitioner researchers as part of their own professional development. Educational psychologists routinely use observation as part of the statutory assessment process for children with SEND and for the holistic assessment of children and young people for non-statutory purposes. Observational data collected in these contexts informs teaching and learning and guides decisions about interventions that might be put in place. However, observation also offers an important research tool.

Observation and research: Why look and listen?

There are several reasons why observation has been a well-used method within educational research. First, observation offers a direct window into how people behave in particular settings and situations. As Cohen et al. (2018: 542) note, the researcher is given the opportunity 'to gather first-hand, live data *in situ* from naturally occurring social situations'. In other words, it gives direct access to what people actually do rather than what they say they do. This has the potential to shed light on different and additional information from that which is gathered using a questionnaire or interview which relies on people's memories and perceptions. Observation also allows the researcher to see and understand the broader contextual factors that may impact a given situation. In a classroom setting, for example, the physical layout, the demographic make-up of the group, the nature of social interactions, the pedagogical context, and the support structures available to learners may all impact on learning outcomes and how particular individuals behave in that setting.

Second, what might broadly be defined as 'observation' covers a wide range of specific practices. Observation can be structured or unstructured, participant or non-participant, and provide qualitative or quantitative data. The settings within which observation takes place, and the range of research foci to which it can be applied, vary greatly. In educational research, observational settings typically include early childhood centres, school classrooms, playgrounds, corridors, halls and staffrooms. Among our students, other settings have included hospital schools, breakfast clubs and residential settings for adults with learning difficulties. This makes observation suitable for a wide variety of research situations and aims. For example, observation can be used for description, comparison, evaluation, awareness raising, problem-solving or documenting change over time. This makes it a versatile research tool. Indeed, Burton et al. (2014: 117) suggest that it offers 'one of the most flexible means of conducting a research study'.

What can be observed?

It goes without saying that observational studies focus on the observable. But what does this mean, and what does it include and exclude? First, 'the observable' refers to behaviour that you can see or hear – in other words, the specific actions that people take. It includes what people do, what they say, and any body and paralanguage associated with those actions. Note that we can't see thoughts, feelings or intentions; these happen inside the psychologist's proverbial black box. Of course, we often make inferences about thoughts, feelings or intentions based on the behaviour we observe. This is what we are doing whenever we read someone's body language. When someone smiles, we infer that they are happy. When they frown, we infer that they are sad, or perhaps uncertain or confused. However, while we can be sure that someone smiled (or frowned) because we saw it, we can never be 100 per cent sure of the meaning or intention behind that behaviour. This is where broadening the focus of the observation to include environmental factors is important for some observational studies. This might include maps of the physical setting, notes about the social and pedagogical contexts, and information on any supports that are available to learners within that setting. These contextual data help the researcher to make sense of the behaviours observed.

In educational settings, observation is often used as a way of learning about what is happening in a particular setting for a particular learner or group of learners. The focus could be academic, social or behavioural. Observation offers a useful tool for gathering comparative data – for example, allowing comparisons between two different learners or for the same learner over time. We illustrate with some simple example questions that could be answered through observation. Note that the distinction between social, academic, behavioural is somewhat arbitrary. All of these questions require focusing on observable behaviour.

Social:

- How often does *pupil x* initiate a social interaction with another child during the morning play break?
- How many different children does *pupil x* interact with during a set activity or period of time?
- How long does each social interaction last?

Academic:

- How many different children use a particular pedagogical support during a set activity?
- How long does *pupil x* work independently on a set academic task?
- How much written work does *pupil x* produce during an unassisted writing task versus an assisted writing task?

Behavioural:

- How does *pupil x* go about initiating social interactions with another child during the morning play break?
- How does *pupil x* engage with this maths task?
- How often does *pupil x* engage in [named specific behaviour]?

You may have noticed that some of these questions focus on how many/how often, others focus on how long, and others focus simply on how. In other words, some focus on frequency of behaviour, some on duration and some more broadly on how events play out over time. These different foci require different observational approaches. This is what we turn to next.

Structured versus unstructured observation

As is the case for interviews, observations can vary across a continuum from structured to unstructured and the degree of structure will be determined by your research questions and aims. At one end of the continuum are **structured observations**. They are suitable for situations where the researcher knows exactly what aspects and behaviours are to be observed. They are defined in advance, along with the length of the observation period, the frequency of the observation points and details of the recording system that will be used (sometimes known as the coding system). This requires developing an observation schedule which is then used to record data during the observation. Structured observations produce quantitative (numerical) data and typically feature in studies that have a narrow, behavioural focus where the aim is to quantify something.

At the other end of the continuum are **unstructured observations**. They are not predetermined in the same way that structured observations are and therefore allow a much broader focus in terms of the sorts of information that is recorded. This makes them suitable for exploratory or descriptive research that aims to produce a more holistic account of what takes place in a particular setting. Unstructured observations produce qualitative (word) data and are typically used in ethnographic-type research. They are sometimes referred to as narrative observations.

Semi-structured observations describe situations that include both structured and unstructured elements. They are common in educational settings where there is a specific focus but where the researcher also wants broader, contextual information such as the details of the physical, pedagogical or social environment, or descriptions of sequences of events. This qualitative data can be invaluable when it comes to making sense of the quantitative data. And as Palaiologou (2019) notes, while semi-structured observations always have some specific aims and objectives, they also 'always entail an element of openness to capture the unpredicted, unexpected events that might happen' (p. 153).

Researcher role

Different research texts describe the range of possible research roles slightly differently but all can be placed along a continuum from complete participant to complete observer. As a **complete participant** the researcher immerses themselves within a particular setting; in other words, they become a member of the group being observed. This role typically features in ethnographic research (see Chapter 9) and has been widely used in the field of anthropology (Cohen et al., 2018). Note that in this context, those being observed may be unaware that research is taking place. This is to avoid people changing their behaviour as a result of knowing that they are being observed, which threatens the validity of the data gathered. This, of course, raises some serious ethical questions as it involves deception and participants have not given informed voluntary consent. Indeed, the lengthy legal battle led by a number of women in England against former members of the London Metropolitan police who formed romantic relationships with these women as part of an undercover surveillance of several protest movements provides an extreme example of participant observation that is ethically untenable.

At the other end of the continuum is the **complete observer**. Here, again, those being researched may be unaware that they are being observed. While this means that participants' behaviour is not influenced by the observer, it also means that no data is gathered from the insider perspective (Mukherji and Albon, 2015). This role is typically adopted in psychological research and can take place in either natural or laboratory settings. Either way, the researcher is unobtrusive and does not interact at all with those being observed. In natural settings, the observer aims to blend in with the environment in order to be invisible and therefore not influence people's behaviour. An example you may be familiar with is studies of superstition where a ladder is propped up over the footpath in a busy pedestrian area and the observer, seated discretely on a nearby bench, records how many people step around the ladder rather than walk under it. In laboratory settings, the complete observer is often located behind a one-way mirror. Many observational studies of child development have used this approach.

Example

This weblink (https://tinyurl.com/2b43sxh2) will take you to a short video clip (2.5 minutes) that illustrates a well-known observational laboratory experiment with babies, called The Hanging Cliff experiment. It was used to learn about 'social referencing' (when a child looks towards the parent to gauge which emotions and actions are appropriate in an uncertain situation). The clip shows the laboratory set up that was developed for this observational study.

Participant as observer describes the situation where the researcher spends a considerable amount of time in the research setting and is part of the group or setting being observed. In these situations, the participants know that the observer is undertaking research. One advantage of this approach is that it allows the researcher to see and understand the various contextual factors that influence behaviour and also how events or situations evolve over time. This allows a more holistic view than is achieved as a non-participant observer.

The **observer as participant** is located within the setting but for limited periods of time. As with participant as observer, those being observed know that the person is undertaking research but the researcher's involvement in the activities being observed is much less compared to participant as observer. The observer is not part of the group and will typically be observing from a distance. This makes it easier for the observer to remain objective but may also mean that they lack the interpretive insight that those who are more deeply immersed in the setting bring to their observation.

Note that published research studies often simply distinguish between participant and non-participant observer but we include the information above as a way of highlighting that levels of participation range across a continuum from complete immersion to complete detachment, as illustrated in Figure 8.1.

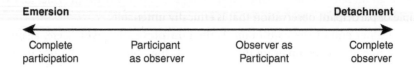

Figure 8.1 Researcher role continuum

Participant observation is common in classroom and playground situations and can be a good option for practitioner researchers. Non-participant observation, where the researcher is physically present in the setting but has less direct interaction with those being observed, is more common for student researchers. In the example below, the role of the researcher falls somewhere between participant as observer and observer as participant but falls closer to the former.

Research example

In their Australian study with four- and five-year-olds, Breathnach et al. (2018) wanted to learn more about strategies that disrupt traditional adult–child power relations within schools. The researcher, who was not a member of staff, joined the children in their normal day-to-day activities. However, she intentionally did not behave in ways expected of adults; for example, she sat on the floor with the children rather than on a chair and if asked a question by another child, she assumed a stance of ignorance and deferred to the expertise of the other children. The interactions were video recorded for subsequent analysis to identify which strategies resulted in greater child control and input.

Recording observational data

So far, we have learned that observations can vary in their degree of structure and how the observer is positioned in relation to those being observed. There are also different ways of recording observational data, each being suitable for a specific sort of observation. Below we present some of the methods most commonly used in educational settings. We start with descriptive or narrative methods that are typically used in unstructured observations before moving to the systematic methods used for structured observations. Note that in reality it may be an adaptation or combination of methods that best suits a particular research purpose. The case study presented later in this chapter illustrates how one student used event recording alongside descriptive notes.

Descriptive methods

Descriptive methods involve the researcher writing down exactly what they see and hear during the observation period. This might include who says what to who, who does what, who goes where, what happens next, and so on. They produce detailed narrative accounts that capture both verbal and non-verbal information as well as how events play out over time. Descriptive records might also include: a description of physical setting, recorded as a map; pen portraits of particular children; or chronological information where the time is noted alongside particular events. If social interactions between those being observed is of interest, then other diagrammatic representations such as sociograms might also be appropriate. Field notes might also include the researcher's reflections on what they observed, or notes on any issues or events that may have influenced what was observed.

Descriptive records are therefore good for gaining a detailed description of what is happening in a specific setting (or for a specific child) across time. This approach generates qualitative data and is appropriate for exploratory research where defined observational categories cannot yet be established. One advantage of this approach is that little advance preparation or training is needed. There are no complicated schedules to follow and no timekeeping is required; the observer simply records what they see and hear as it occurs. Importantly, it is observable behaviour, and not the observer's interpretation of that behaviour, that must remain the key focus. Of course, the observer may want to add their reflections or speculate about the meaning of the behaviour, but the observer needs to differentiate clearly between what was seen and heard, and what meaning might (or might not) be attached to that. Figure 8.2 presents a simple template that can be adapted for a descriptive record.

Location and context:		
Observation focus:		
Who is being observed:		
Date:	Start time:	Finish time:
Time	Descriptive notes	Additional information (reflections/questions/possible interpretations)

Figure 8.2 Example descriptive record template

One disadvantage of descriptive records is that their unstructured nature means that the data cannot easily be used for comparative purposes. Additionally, although no specific preparation or training is required, educational settings are busy places and the speed at which events occur can make it hard to keep track of all of the events or factors that are salient to a particular observation. Consequently, something important might be missed (Wragg, 2012). This is why some researchers enlist the aid of video-recording technology. Many experienced observers also develop their own abbreviations or short-hand to help with this issue.

Systematic methods

Event recording in its simplest form involves observing a single person and focuses on a single, predetermined and clearly defined behaviour. It is used when the researcher wants to determine the frequency of an event or behaviour. To do this, a record of the event or behaviour is taken each and every time it occurs within the specified observa-tion period, often using a simple tally chart. The raw data is therefore the total number of times the event or behaviour occurred during the observation period. This approach is useful when the focus of the observation is an easily identified, discrete behaviour or event.

Interval recording, sometimes also referred to as interval-sampling, is when the observation schedule is divided into a number of discrete intervals of equal duration. For example, a one-hour observation might be divided into 12 five-minute intervals. The observer records whether or not the specified event or behaviour occurs *at any point* during the current interval. It differs from event recording in that if the event or behaviour occurs multiple times during the same interval, it is still only recorded once. The raw data is therefore the number of intervals within which the event or behaviour occurred. This is often expressed as a percentage.

Time-sampling is similar to interval recording in that the observation period is divided into equal intervals. It differs from interval recording in that the behaviour of interest is only recorded if it occurs at the end of the specified interval. In other words, the observer looks at the target child only at the end of the interval. The raw data is therefore the number of intervals within which the event or behaviour is occurring at the specified observation point. Again, this can be expressed as a percentage. Note that while event recording provides an exact count of the specified event or behaviour, interval and time-sampling methods provide an estimate rather than the exact frequency. This makes them suitable for high-frequency behaviours that are difficult to count, or when it's dif-ficult to determine when a behaviour starts and finishes.

For all three methods, data is recorded on an observation schedule that is prepared prior to the observation and on which the behaviour of interest is clearly defined. For interval and time-sampling methods, the observer also needs a timer to keep track of the intervals. We also strongly recommend that you pilot your observation schedule. You may not know enough about the frequency of an event or behaviour before an obser-vation to choose an appropriate interval length. If your chosen interval is too long you will get an underestimate, and if it's too short you will get an overestimate. You therefore need to check this by testing it. As noted in the previous chapter on interviews, gath-ering quality data also depends on practising your method until you feel confident and competent with it.

Systematic methods have several advantages which make them suitable for the aims and objectives of some studies. First, they provide very specific information and are easily repeatable. This makes them suitable for the early stages of a study where you want to establish baseline information or for situations where you want comparative data in relation to a specific behaviour or event. Also, the system you design could include more than one event or behaviour and focus on more than one child or group, thus offering greater time efficiency than focusing on a single child or event. Additionally, the quantitative data that is generated is more easily organised and analysed than the qualitative data generated by descriptive methods.

One challenge specific to systematic observations is that of 'operationalising' the behaviour(s) to be observed. This refers to formulating a very narrow, focused definition that would allow two different people to produce the same results if they both undertook the same observation at the same time. It's harder than it might first appear. The scenario below and the activity that follows help illustrate this.

Scenario

Pupil X, who is seven years old, attends a mainstream school and has been diagnosed as having ASD. Her teacher has noticed that she often sits or walks alone during unstructured breaks. He wants to introduce a short social skills intervention that will promote greater social engagement during these times. First, he needs to establish some baseline data about the current levels of social engagement. A simple event-recording procedure is suitable for this. The behaviours of interest are 'initiates a social interaction with another pupil' and 'responds to a social initiation from another pupil'. The time period of interest is the unstructured playtime during the second half of the lunch break. The initial event-recording schedule for this scenario is presented in Table 8.1.

Table 8.1 First event-recording schedule for the scenario

Pupil X	Playground observation	
Date:	Time: 12:30–12:55	Total
Behaviour 1: Initiates social interaction with another pupil		
Behaviour 2: Responds to a social interaction with another pupil		

The teacher recruits two teacher trainees who are currently on placement at the school to undertake the observations for a week. Each observes separately and then they compare their tallies. The observation schedule has not been piloted but the teacher talks it through with the trainees.

Activity 8.1

Before reading on, consider your answers to the questions below.

1   On day one, both observers found that the total number of instances of behaviour 1 was greater than those of behaviour 2. However, their total tallies for each behaviour were quite different. How could this be explained?
2   What is one thing that could be done to increase the reliability of the data collected?

In this scenario, 'Initiates a social interaction' is a broad definition that is open to interpretation. Does a 'social interaction' require a verbal exchange or could non-verbal behaviours such as gestures also count? Does making eye contact or smiling at another pupil constitute a social interaction? Does an interaction only count if it results in ongoing engagement? Producing a narrow enough definition that will allow two observers to come up with the same results requires identifying some discrete behaviours that are indicative of the broader behaviour of interest. Pilot testing is a good way of checking that this has been achieved.

After discussing the results of the first observation with the two teacher trainees, the teacher modified the observation schedule so that each main behaviour of interest was broken down into a smaller set of more discrete behaviours, as illustrated in Table 8.2. On day two, the tallies for each behaviour were either the same or differed by only one. Extending the observation period for ten days rather than just five would increase the generalisability of the data collected.

Table 8.2   Revised event-recording schedule for behaviour 1

Pupil X:	Playground observation	
Date:	Time: 12:30–12:55pm	
Behaviour 1: Initiates social interaction with another pupil		Total
Physically approaches and comes within two metres of another pupil or group of pupils		
Makes eye contact with one or more pupils		
Uses a non-verbal gesture to attract the attention of another pupil or group of pupils		
Starts a conversation with another pupil		

Another disadvantage of systematic methods is that the focus on narrowly defined behaviours means that contextual information is not recorded. This makes it difficult to speculate about why an event or behaviour has occurred and why the approach might be used as one part of a larger study. As Mukherji and Albon (2015) point out, a combination of descriptive and systematic methods will provide both depth and breadth, thus offering a more holistic picture than that provided by a single method on its own. The case study below and Table 8.3 illustrate how one student used event recording but also collected some descriptive data.

Case study 8.1

Tania volunteered in a special school for children with learning difficulties and had noticed that many of children appeared to have very short attention spans. These children often left their seats to wander around the room, sometimes distracting others and frequently not completing set tasks. Tania wanted to know if introducing a short daily physical exercise routine halfway through the first learning block would help children to stay on task for longer. To do this, she needed to gather some pre- and post-exercise data. She developed an observation schedule that combined elements from systematic and descriptive approaches. For the systematic element, she undertook a frequency count of two predetermined behaviours likely to be indicative of a child being off task. Namely: leaves seat to wander around the classroom; distracts others from the task at hand (either verbally or physically). She also recorded whether or not they completed the set task within the time allocated. Alongside this she took descriptive field notes of any contextual information that she thought might be impacting on what she observed on any given day. Table 8.3 is illustrative of the observation schedule that Tania used. To make the observation more manageable, she focused on only two children. She undertook her observations at the same time each day for ten consecutive school days.

Table 8.3 Exemplar observation schedule

Observation number:			Date:	
Frequency of disengagement	Before activity		After activity	
	Child A_____	Child B	Child A_____	Child B
Leaves seat/ wanders around class	*### //*	*////*		
Distracts other pupils (verbally or physically)	*////*	*### ///*		

Observation number:			Date:
Completes set tasks	No	No	

Pre-activity field notes:	Time:
Very warm day	9:00
All children very quiet at beginning of lesson	
Some children (including focus children) looking around room, out of window and at floor - prompted by TA to watch and listen to teacher as she talked through the task	9:05
Some pupils given warnings for shouting out answers rather than raising hand (including Child B)	9:12
Classroom next door now playing loud music - many children looking around for source; some children covering ears	9:15
Child B starts singing out loud until reprimanded	9:16
About half the class appear to be engaged in set task	9:20
Child A leaves seat (to request assistance from the TA)	9:25

Issues to consider in observational research

We now turn to a number of important issues that need to be taken into consideration when planning your observational study. The first three relate to research rigour or trustworthiness: they impact the reliability of the data you collect and the validity of your findings. The last two are planning and management issues and serve to highlight one of the disadvantages of observational studies: namely, that they can be time consuming.

The presence of an observer

The presence of an observer (or recording equipment) will almost certainly have an impact on what is observed. Studies have shown that even when an observer is being as unobtrusive as possible, those being observed react to the knowledge that they are being observed. This is often referred to as the Hawthorne effect – named after a 1920s American study of factory workers that found that no matter what changes to the environment were introduced, or how the observation was conducted, productivity went up. In an educational context, the presence of someone new is likely to garner some interest, even if just initially. The challenge is that an observer can never be 100 per cent sure of the extent of that impact. Wragg (2012) points out that the extent of impact on those being observed will vary depending on a number of factors such as the observer's age, gender or ethnicity. Perceived status also plays a part. Many teachers will attest to the uncharacteristic behaviour of some pupils during school inspections. On the other hand, if a setting frequently has visitors, then the presence of someone new is less of a novelty and will have less impact. The important thing is to be aware that your presence will have an impact and to consider actions that you can take to minimise this. For example, if you are a non-participant observer, then sit wherever makes you as unobtrusive as possible. Spending time in the setting prior to your actual observations so that learners become accustomed to your presence will also reduce the impact of your presence.

Observer bias

Observer bias refers to factors associated with the observer that affect the reliability of the data collected and how it is interpreted. If you have two observers who are using the same observation schedule in the same setting at the same time but produce different results, then observer bias is likely to be at play. Note, however, that factors such as tiredness, inattention or insufficient experience in using the observation schedule may also contribute to inaccuracies in the data that is recorded. Observer bias is a greater risk in unstructured observations where what an observer focuses on and takes note of may be influenced by their lived experience and who they are. As Mukherji and Albon (2015: 147) point out, 'culture, class, religion, level of education and past life experiences all contribute to the way we interpret what we see'. This is why it's important to focus on what you see and hear whilst avoiding evaluations, judgements or speculations.

Generalisability

With both descriptive and systematic recording methods, it is possible that the sample you collect is not representative. This is because there are many extraneous variables that might influence someone's behaviour on any given day. These could be internal factors such as illness or hunger, external factors such as having had an argument with a friend, or environmental factors such as it being a very hot or cold day. For school-based research, the time of the year will also have an impact. An observation during the week before the Christmas break is likely to yield different results from one taken part way though a school term. The issue is mitigated by undertaking observations on multiple occasions or of longer duration, which minimises the effect of any single extraneous factor on the overall results. In other words, the larger the observation sample, the more confident you can be about the conclusions that you draw.

Observation is a time-consuming process

As noted above, the reliability of observation data is strengthened by undertaking multiple observations. Fieldwork might therefore extend over a considerable period. This is one factor that makes observation a time-consuming process. Additionally, reliable and valid observations also require an observation schedule that is fit for purpose and an observer who is proficient in using it. Designing the schedule, piloting it and gaining experience using it all take time. Time can be a particular challenge for practitioner researchers who want to undertake research in their work settings because they still have their day-to-day work responsibilities to manage as well. This does not mean ruling out observation but you might need to apply some creativity. One busy teacher moved counters from one pocket to another as a way of recording the frequency of a specific behaviour of one of her pupils. Finally, you need to factor in additional contingency time because factors out of your control will inevitably impede your plans. Inclement weather might mean a playground observation cannot take place; the particular pupil you planned to observe may be absent that day; the pupil might be present but the teacher points out that s/he is having an 'off-day' and is therefore not displaying typical behaviour; nobody informed you about the whole-school sports or literacy event that day. These factors need to be taken into consideration when planning your study to ensure that your plans are realistic within the available time.

Ethical considerations

Cohen et al. (2018: 562) state that 'Like other forms of data collection in the human sciences, observation is not a morally neutral enterprise.' They are referring to some of the ethical issues that are particular to observation. For example, if you are observing just one pupil in a class, do you need parental permission for all pupils? How do you observe whilst minimising disruption to the normal routines and activities? What if you are in a class and observe something that you think requires intervention? Do you step in if you see a child being bullied? Do you intervene in an altercation between two children? Do you assist someone who clearly needs some help? As a non-participant observer you might plan to remain detached from what is going on, but you may well find yourself in a situation that requires professional judgement and a change from your intended stance of non-intervention. Planning for these possibilities prior to the observation will help you to make good judgements on the day. You also need to be clear in advance how you will manage situations where children engage with you. Particularly if you are observing in a class of younger children who are accustomed to different adults coming and going over the course of the school day, there is a good chance that you will be approached. It may just be a matter of curiosity if you are a new presence, but it's just as likely to involve a request for assistance, a shoelace that needs tying, a nose that needs blowing, an outer layer of clothing that needs removing, or a word that a child is struggling to read or spell. Remember that children have a right to know who you are and why you are there. This will also help them to understand how they should treat you while you are there.

Planning your observational study

There are some key decisions that need to be made when planning your observational study. Each should be guided by your research question and aims. Once you are clear about the key purpose and focus of your observation, the rest should fall into place and you should be able to answer each of the questions below. Remember that there is no single best way to engage in observational research; rather, each approach has its strengths and limitations.

- Who do I need to observe?
- What sort of observation is appropriate (structured/unstructured)?
- Will I be a participant or a non-participant observer?
- Where and when will observations take place?
- How many observations do I need to undertake to be confident about my data?
- How long will each observation take?
- How will I record and analyse data?
- Have I prepared and piloted a suitable observation schedule?
- If using a structured observation, have I clearly defined the focus behaviour(s)?
- What ethical issues may arise and how will I address them?
- How will the observations complement other data-collection methods that I may be employing?

Checkpoint 8.1

- If you have no preconceived ideas about what you are going to find, then opt for descriptive field notes rather than a structured observation schedule.
- If you are not sure which categories to use or how to define behaviours or events, you will need to spend time in the setting first.
- Stay focused on observable behaviour while also recording any other contextual information that you think might be useful.
- If you need to develop a structured observation schedule, pilot it and practise until you are proficient in its use.
- Anticipate potential problems and decide in advance what actions you might take to mitigate them.
- Increase the reliability of data by undertaking repeat observations or observations of longer duration.

Chapter summary

This chapter has focused on observation and what it can contribute to the research process. We have learned that it has a long history in educational research, particularly in relation to child development. Observations, like interviews, can take a range of forms depending on the degree of structure, the position adopted by the observer in relation to those being observed and the tools used to collect data. Additionally, they can be undertaken in a range of settings and produce both quantitative and qualitative data. This makes them a versatile set of methods that can be applied to a wide range of research purposes.

The particular approach you adopt will be determined by the extent to which it enables you to answer your research question and by the relative advantages and disadvantages of any particular observational method. Successful observation also requires you to consider the range of issues that impact the quality of data you gather and how ethical questions can best be addressed. In the next chapter, we move beyond more traditional approaches to research to consider how methods might be adapted to enable the participation of a wider range of learners whose voices may otherwise remain absent or marginalised.

Recommended reading

- Chapter 26 in Cohen, L., Manion, L. and Morrison, K. (2018) *Research Methods in Education*, 8th edn. London: Routledge.

Outline: This chapter on observation expands on some of the ideas presented here but also covers additional territory such as the observation of 'critical incidents'. It would be particularly beneficial for anyone planning to undertake structured observations. The table and figures also provide useful examples and summaries.

- Palaiologou, I. (2019) *Child Observation: A Guide for Students of Early Childhood*, 4th edn. London: Sage.

Outline: This book offers a practical guide to planning and undertaking observations of children in an educational setting. Although the examples and case studies are specific to the early childhood context, they can easily be adapted to a broader range of learners and contexts.

9

ADAPTING METHODOLOGY TO SPECIAL AND INCLUSIVE EDUCATION

━━━━━━━━━ **Chapter objectives** ━━━━━━━━━

By the end of this chapter you will:

- ✓ Know the key features of a range of some innovative/adaptive approaches to research in special and inclusive education
- ✓ Understand some common challenges to inclusive participation within research in this field and how to go about overcoming them
- ✓ Have explored examples of ways in which data-collection methods can be adapted to a specific context/participant in special and inclusive education
- ✓ Understand how to balance ethical considerations with the importance of enabling participation in research

Introduction

We have now explored a wide variety of methodological approaches and accompanying methods of data collection across Chapters 6 to 8. It is our experience that, for the vast majority of students in special and inclusive education, these methods are highly suitable to meeting their research aims. However, some of you who now have a topic of research in mind may be thinking that the approaches and methods we have explored thus far may not be entirely applicable to research in your area of interest. This is a common issue in our field, primarily as a result of the aforementioned uniqueness of many of the contexts in which research in special and inclusive education takes place.

There are often specific challenges to data collection in our field. For example, it is neither valid nor ethical to conduct a formal standardised interview with a participant who experiences significant challenges with verbal communication. It is vital that an effective researcher ensures that the methodology they select for use in their study is appropriate in relation to the needs and abilities of the participants. Yet we would advocate not shying away from involving participants who may have a lot to offer the research simply because it is more difficult to design effective data-collection tools for them. We hope that this chapter begins to open up a range of adaptable approaches to you, with the aim of supporting more researchers to employ inclusive methodology to support innovative research studies in our field.

The approaches explored in this chapter are heavily weighted towards enabling the involvement of children and adults identified with special educational needs to participate in research. This is because, in our experience, they are the most frequent groups for whom researchers struggle to design effective data-collection methods. Some of the methods we will highlight have been adapted from methods employed by researchers in other fields. It should be noted that you are highly unlikely to be able to take these approaches off the shelf and use them directly in your study; they are likely to need further adaptation to reflect the uniqueness of the context in which you are hoping to conduct research.

This chapter will begin by exploring (auto)ethnography, a further example of a methodological approach that is seeing increasing use in the field of special and inclusive education. This will give an additional choice to the range of methodological approaches presented in Chapter 6. The remainder of the chapter will then be dedicated to exploring innovative, multisensory data-collection methods. These methods expand the range we have already explored in Chapters 7 and 8.

At this point, it is important to remind yourself of the difference between methodological approach and data-collection methods, as explored in relation to mixed methods in Chapter 6 and in Figure 9.1.

Figure 9.1 Thinking process for identifying paradigms

The first approach that we will explore in this chapter, (auto)ethnography, is an example of a methodological approach, represented in the third stage of the process outlined in Figure 9.1. The remainder of the approaches that we explore in this chapter are examples of data-collection methods, represented in the fourth stage of the figure.

Ethnography in special and inclusive education

Ethnography as a methodological approach is not a new phenomenon in research; it is not especially new to the field of education either. Examples of ethnographic research in education have been plentiful in the last 20 years or so. However, its use in special and inclusive education often comes with particular challenges/considerations, which can act as barriers to effective implementation with regard to special and inclusive contexts. Certainly, the autoethnographical approach is less common in our field but we are seeing more students successfully, and often bravely, endeavour to undertake this approach to their research.

Ethnography is simply defined as 'the study of a culture or cultures that a group of people share' (Check and Schutt, 2011: 309). At a basic level, an ethnographic study focuses on observation, of people/social interactions within a very specific context. As Hammersley (1985) identifies, the aim is to 'get inside' the way in which a group of people sees the world and begin to understand their realities. In order to do this, at least one specific data-collection method must always be employed within an ethnographic methodological approach, that of participant observation. It will be useful for you to review the section on participant observation in Chapter 8 if you are interested in ethnography.

You may be thinking that the aim of most empirical research in special and inclusive education, indeed in education in general, is to 'get inside' the thoughts of the teachers/students to form a new understanding. We often hope to do that via a case study or action research, for example. Of course, that is a valid point, but the difference with ethnographic research lies in the role of the researcher. A researcher undertaking an ethnographic study may only truly be able to 'get inside' the social dynamics of interest by fully immersing themselves in the context of the research. It is this immersion in the context of interest that makes this methodological approach particularly attractive to some researchers in the field of special and inclusive education.

As we have explored previously in this book, many of the contexts of interest in special and inclusive education display elements of uniqueness. There is an argument that the only way to truly understand the nuances that form this uniqueness is to immerse yourself in it. Thus, the ethnographic approach can allow some researchers to meet more innovative research aims than traditional methods will allow. To explore this further, it is best to share a successful example of ethnographic research in a special and inclusive context.

Case study 9.1

Ethnography

Davis, J., Watson, N. and Cunningham-Burley, S. (2017) Disabled children, ethnography and unspoken understandings: The collaborative construction of diverse identities. Chapter 7 in: P.M. Christensen and A. James (eds) *Research with Children: Perspectives and Practices*, 3rd edn. London: Routledge.

This chapter provides a rich exploration of the benefits and challenges of employing an ethnographic methodological approach in the setting of a special school in Scotland. The authors describe how they immersed themselves in the school for more than six weeks in order to gain an in-depth understanding of communication styles between the adults and children. John, the ethnographer/researcher, identified that he undertook a range of roles during his participant observation, from friend/helper to authoritarian.

John discusses his experience of working with Scott, a student who John had assumed was non-verbal as he used hand gestures/symbols to communicate with him. After having been in the school for a while, John asked Scott to complete a picture story with him and during the activity Scott began to speak about his family. John realised that he had mistakenly categorised Scott as non-verbal and noted the importance of the ethnographic approach in allowing him to build a richer understanding of the participants in his study. Ultimately, the authors were able to successfully challenge the perception that children who are disabled are not capable of social action and they constructed complex understandings of the children's lives and identities.

This is an important example as it highlights the benefits of considering an ethnographic approach in special and inclusive education. The complexities of the individuals we may involve in research often take a significant amount of time and interaction to de-tangle and the ethnographic approach can afford this.

Autoethnography in special and inclusive education

Many of the principles associated with an ethnographic approach are present within autoethnography, those of participant observation being central to the approach and the notion of immersing oneself in the context of the research. However, the key difference with autoethnography is that the context is one's own experiences rather than those of others.

Autoethnography can be defined as 'a genre of writing that places the self of the researcher and/or narrator within a social context' (Reed-Danahay, 2017: 144). The autoethnographer immerses themselves in the context of their own lived experiences, primarily in order to explore the cultural/political understandings within those experiences, thus enabling further identification of how these understandings translate to wider educational contexts. Autoethnographers often make use of various forms of written data – for example, memoirs, diary entries, narrative prose and critical reflections – which form a catalogue of experiences that are analysed via documentary analysis. (This will be explored further in Chapter 10.)

Autoethnography as a methodological approach in our field is still relatively unusual in our experience, particularly at master's level. However, it can be very suitable for those who have a range of experiences within education that may provide strong material for an in-depth analysis of a concept/topic of interest. An example of a successful autoethnographical study by one of our MA Education students is outlined below.

Case study 9.2

Autoethnography

Whilst completing her MA in Education, Hannah was working as a secondary school science teacher. She had struggled with a range of mental health difficulties throughout her life and felt that, at times, her role as a teacher exacerbated some of these difficulties. Yet Hannah was a very successful teacher and had a strong track record of success in education more generally; she had always achieved high grades at school and was well regarded by her colleagues and students. She was aware of the much-reported link between mental health difficulties and the teaching profession, as well as the increase in mental health needs in the children she worked with.

Hannah was therefore interested to explore the ways in which her lived experiences had enabled her to function successfully in her role as a teacher, despite great challenges to her mental health. Hannah used diary entries and narrative prose to critically analyse her prior experiences in meeting her research aims.

The research experience was often challenging for Hannah; she was forced to confront some challenging memories and experiences in her analysis. Yet her thesis was very successful in identifying her support mechanisms and contributed much to the wider debate on promoting good mental health for the teaching profession, for both policy and practice.

Positives and drawbacks of (auto)ethnography

Arguably the strongest positive of (auto)ethnography is the level of depth in criticism that the approach can support. The researcher is able to fully immerse themselves in the research process; this not only means immersion in the research context, but also in the data. Many (auto)ethnographic studies result in highly successful, critical write-ups, which can provide useful findings that can contribute to wide-ranging debates in the field of special and inclusive education.

However, as with other context-specific research approaches, there are significant issues with generalisability when conducting an ethnographic study. Nevertheless, a researcher hoping to generalise from their research simply would not choose to follow an ethnographic approach in their research design; as was explored in Chapter 6, the particularisation of a context-specific study can be its strength (Flyvbjerg, 2006). (Auto) ethnography is only a suitable choice for researchers who see value in the specificity and particularisation of a single context.

Finally, it should be noted that undertaking an ethnographic study is not a simple task. Most of the methodological approaches explored in Chapter 6 follow a tight structural design; ethnographic studies are generally much more flexible in design. Therefore, a researcher following this approach must keep focused and on task throughout the entire research process; it requires a significant amount of motivation to complete an ethnographic study successfully. It also requires a researcher who has a very strong ability to think and write critically.

The experience can be taxing on the researcher, as can be seen with Hannah's example. Autoethnography can be especially taxing in our field due to the personal, often emotional, nature of the research process. Ethnography can also be taxing on participants, as researchers are often seeking a significant time commitment from participants to enable sufficient immersion by the researcher. The ethical implications are paramount, particularly when considering its use in special and inclusive education.

Finally, a useful question for you to ponder in relation to ethnography in special and inclusive education, for which there is no clear and decisive answer: Can we ever truly understand the experiences of others, especially those who possess special educational needs that result in them viewing the world differently?

Checkpoint 9.1

- Ethnography involves a researcher immersing themselves in the context of interest to gain deeper understandings of a topic/issue of interest.
- Autoethnography involves immersing oneself in their personal reflections/experiences.
- All ethnographic research should, at a minimum, involve participant observation as a data-collection method.
- Ethnographic studies require a researcher to display significant personal motivation and excellent critical analysis skills.

Innovative data-collection methods in special and inclusive education: Multisensory approaches

As identified earlier in this chapter, many of the traditional methods of data collection in the field of education may not be entirely appropriate for use in special and inclusive education.

It may be that you are hoping to work with participants who have limited verbal communication skills, or those who may not respond well to a formalised interview/observational environment. The aim of this section is to provide you with some useful examples of alternative/adapted data-collection methods, which may support you to involve a wider range of participants than is possible with more traditional methodology.

The methods explored in this section are largely inspired by the work of Alison Clark (2011) whose research resulted in the introduction of the Mosaic approach to data collection. This approach was motivated by the desire to involve very young children in research design in a way that takes account of their different competencies and also recognises the importance of the voice of children in research. The methods highlighted by Clark view children as 'co-creators'. In this approach, researchers aim to devise, implement and analyse research with participants, rather than independently of them .

The methods that we highlight, although largely influenced by those explored by Clark, are intended to move beyond the participation of young children and support the involvement of older children and vulnerable adults who may have an identified special educational need or may simply display competencies that are not suited to traditional research methodology. You will notice that these methods move away from the traditional focus on the written/spoken word and more towards multisensory experiences, thereby immediately enabling wider participation from those whose literacy skills are often a barrier to their participation in research. We will explore the following multisensory data-collection methods in the remainder of this chapter:

- Transect walks
- Photography
- Research conversations

Transect walks

Transect walks were first used in the field of international development; they allow people who have difficulties with literacy skills to convey their local knowledge about their immediate surroundings (Hart, 1997). Their particular popularity with research involving children in educational settings has originated due to the natural interest in exploration that children often display.

Transect walks are characterised by structured walks with participants, in a familiar context to them, in order for the researcher to explore specific sociocultural concepts as viewed by the participant(s) (Kirylo, 2020). These contexts are almost always the school/college/other educational institution that the participant(s) attends. The researcher often guides the walk by observing, asking, listening and looking at areas of interest to one or both parties. They frequently support the researcher to elicit and further examine people's experiences, successfully enabling the development of new knowledge and understanding.

The key advantage of using transect walks in the field of special and inclusive education is that they often provide a less threatening environment for participants, who may be particularly aware of a power differential between themselves and the researcher, due to their additional needs and vulnerability. Therefore, they can be very successful when used to collect data from children, adults with a range of special educational needs and vulnerable participants, for example those having experienced trauma. The walks take place in a context that is very familiar to the participants and often very unfamiliar to the researcher. The power differential is therefore greatly reduced. This can mean that participants feel more comfortable and able to share their insights with the researcher, resulting in higher-quality data collection. This is also beneficial for participants who may have limited communication skills; the focus is on navigating through the process of the walk and not so much on verbal communication. The researcher may more readily pick up on both verbal and non-verbal cues than if a traditional interview was conducted in an unfamiliar room, with a table in between researcher and participant.

In order for a transect walk to be successful, it is vital that the walk enables the researcher to gather data that is relevant to their area of interest. You must be confident that the environment itself, or the talk that will be generated via the walk, will explore areas that are relevant to your research aims. It is therefore helpful to identify specific verbal prompts and areas to walk through that will support you to discuss areas that are beneficial to your research. The flexibility of this data-collection method can be its downfall if not planned or executed effectively.

Case study 9.3

Transect walks

Kartik, an MA student, was interested in exploring the ways in which the university at which he was studying supported physically disabled students to access and participate in various aspects of student life. He wanted to access the perspectives of physically disabled students, to find out whether any specific barriers to their participation existed within the university. The aim of his study was to identify how successful the university was in enabling effective participation for physically disabled students.

Kartik decided to employ transect walks as a data-collection method with five physically disabled students enrolled in a range of courses across the university. The transect walks were chosen because they enabled Kartik to gain a real-life view of physical barriers to access during the process of the walk. They also enabled additional perspectives to be gained on issues related to participation, drawing on verbal data that was gathered from the conversations that he had with the participants whilst on the walks. The university campus was a very familiar environment to the participants. Kartik therefore found that the participants were willing to engage in and, at times, lead the conversations between them, resulting in rich data that supported his research aims.

The following research foci, in the field of special and inclusive education, have also successfully employed transect walks as a data-collection method:

- To explore the impact of accessing higher education on the life chances of an ex-offender (walk around the college that the participant now attends)
- To identify the social positioning of looked after children in Year 6 within a primary school (walks with various children of that year group around the school)
- To explore the notion of 'community cohesion' for vulnerable adults accessing local education classes in a London borough (walks with vulnerable participants around their local community)

Photography

The use of photography in special and inclusive education is rising in popularity. It can be a powerful data-collection method in studies that are interested in exploring a wide range of concepts and issues in our field. Imagery, in general, often unlocks viewpoints that may not otherwise have been easily accessed by the researcher; photographs often evoke an emotional response, which it can be powerful for the researcher to explore. Photography can be particularly appropriate for use when conducting research with participants who have language barriers, both spoken and written. This is because photographs can give participants a powerful new language through which to make their thoughts and feelings known (Clark, 2004).

Most studies employing photography as a data-collection method ask participants to take pictures of things, often people and places, that are important to them (Hill, 2014). Enabling the participants to have ownership over the camera, and the resulting imagery, is important as it ensures that the images accurately reflect the participants' social understanding in the context of interest. The resulting photographs can be analysed via interpretive phenomenological analysis (IPA), which is explored further in Chapter 10. They can also provide the scaffolding required to undertake follow-up research conversations with participants, explored in the following section.

Case study 9.4

Photography

Hill, L. (2014) 'Some of it I haven't told anybody else': Using photo elicitation to explore the experiences of secondary school education from the perspective of young people with a diagnosis of autistic spectrum disorder. *Educational & Child Psychology*, 31(1): 79–89.

Hill made use of photography in her study designed to explore the lived experience of mainstream secondary school for young people with a diagnosis of autistic spectrum disorder (ASD). The photography method was chosen because Hill was seeking to empower

(Continued)

the young people to tell their stories through research tools that would facilitate their engagement with the process. The participants were tasked with taking photographs of aspects of school life that were important to them, these subsequently forming the central focus of what we term 'research conversations' (which are explored in the following section).

Hill deemed it important that the young people had complete control over the camera, so that all the images truly reflected the factors that were important to them rather than being items perceived to be significant by an outsider. Hill found that employing the photography method resulted in strong enthusiasm from the participants. Participants found the method successful, one participant noting, 'It was easier because I could show you what place I was talking about' (Hill, 2014: 87).

Research conversations

'Research conversations' is a term that we will use to denote a method that is generally characterised by two important elements: informality and scaffolding. In research conversations, the researcher is generally happy for the participants to take the lead in the conversations (hence the informality), as this best supports flowing conversation. Crucially, however, research conversations are scaffolded by additional activities and prompting materials to support both extended interactions and focused discussions. These materials could be devised in a range of ways but must be directly relevant to supporting discussion that will meet your research aims.

One of the most successful examples of research conversations being used as a research method with vulnerable children is research conducted by Punch (2009). The aim of Punch's research was to explore children's negotiation of their autonomy at home, at school, at work and at play. She lived for extended periods in Bolivia, the setting of her research, and took an ethnographic approach. She quickly realised that standardised participant observation and interviewing alone would not allow her to adequately access children's understanding in relation to her research aim. She therefore employed a range of tasks with the children in order to better access their understanding. These tasks included children writing diaries, taking photographs, drawing pictures, completing worksheets and creating spider diagrams and activity tables. The benefit of using this combination of data-collection methods was not always in the results of the tasks themselves but in the resulting conversations. Punch termed these conversations 'informal interviews' but we will use the term 'research conversations' to best describe these interactions.

Research conversations can be a highly successful research method in the field of special and inclusive education because many participants in our field may not respond well to a typical, structured interview situation. They may feel intimidated and/or exposed by the formality of a traditional interview due to social anxieties or language development issues. However, when scaffolding materials are used and the participant is able to focus their talk on these materials and to some extent direct the flow of the interview, the researcher is often able to collect data of a much higher quality. The flexibility and adaptability of this method makes it very suitable for use in a wide range of research within our field. As explored in Punch's study, research conversations can be scaffolded by a wide variety of tasks and other data-collection tools. Figure 9.2 highlights some of these and should provide a useful stimulus for those of you thinking about employing research conversations.

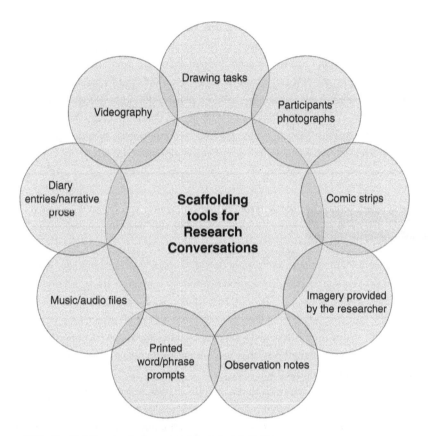

Figure 9.2 Scaffolding tools for research conversations

Case study 9.5

Research conversations

Helen, a PhD student, was interested in exploring the views of children across three mainstream primary schools in the UK with regard to the role of teaching assistants (TAs) in those schools. She was also interested in exploring the social positioning of the children

(Continued)

who worked with TAs regularly. To do this, Helen needed to speak with a range of children across the schools, both those who regularly worked with TAs and those who did not. Much of the focus of this research was sensitive in nature; the participants were all children, many of whom were particularly vulnerable due to their additional needs or apparent lack of social inclusion. It would not have been ethical or valid to ask children who were not socially included about their friends in school. Therefore, Helen adopted scaffolded research conversations with the children.

Before the research conversations took place, Helen employed photography with a sampled group of children in each school. They were asked to take pictures of people and places that were important to them in school. Helen printed a range of their photographs to use as prompts during the research conversations. The photographs from each child almost always showed at least one TA and other children playing during playtime. They provided a gentle way for Helen to ask questions that would access children's understanding in relation to social inclusion and the TA role, resulting in much higher-quality data being gathered than when standardised interviews had been employed during her pilot study.

Checkpoint 9.2

- Multisensory methods are examples of data-collection methods that can be employed within a chosen methodological approach (ethnography, case study, action research).
- All of these methods can be designed to better support participation by vulnerable groups by reducing reliance on literacy skills that traditional research methods require.
- Most multisensory methods achieve success because the power dynamic is different from that in traditional methods; they focus on shaping research alongside participants rather than separately from them.
- Adapting multisensory methods to the abilities of specific groups and to meet specific research aims is vital; they require significant practical and ethical thought in their design. The examples given in this chapter are not intended to be taken off the shelf and used in your research.

Chapter summary

To appropriately summarise this chapter on innovative methodology, it is important that we consider the ethical implications of implementing the examples explored. The ethical considerations discussed in Chapter 4 are all directly relevant to innovative methodology in special and inclusive education. However, the methods explored in this chapter are often accompanied by additional ethical considerations, which are important to highlight.

The methodology explored in this chapter is likely to involve participants who are vulnerable; indeed, many participants will be asked to reflect upon and share experiences that may be sensitive or uncomfortable for them. You must consider how to best support your participants if they become upset during your data-collection process. As a general rule, you should allow your participants to take the lead when implementing one of the approaches explored in this chapter, so that they are more easily able to share information that they are comfortable with and avoid the data-collection process becoming too uncomfortable for them. Additionally, if you are hoping to use photography or other methods that involve taking recordings of children, you must ensure that you consult the policies of the setting that you're working with (for example, school, college or university) so as to ensure that participants' anonymity is protected. You must ensure, for example, that you do not take photographs of looked after children if you are working in a school. Finally, you must have a clear plan for how to store and protect these sensitive data.

Employing the methodology explored in this chapter certainly requires significant thought during the planning and design process. Yet, if thought out successfully, these methods could allow you to take account of the voices of participants who may otherwise have been marginalised from the research process. If you are interested in making use of them, we suggest that you undertake the activity below. We encourage you to think carefully about the methodology and participants specific to your study and to use the example below to scaffold your ethical thinking during the design process.

Activity 9.1

Reflective questions – planning and implementing innovative methodology

Emma, an MA Education student, is interested in exploring the social experiences of children with a diagnosis of autism spectrum disorder (ASD) in a mainstream secondary school in England. Specifically, Emma wants to understand the social experiences of these children during breaktimes to understand their experiences of inclusion in school. Emma is hoping to conduct a case study methodological approach; her data-collection methods will include transect walks with five children identified with ASD and research conversations with these children, scaffolded by images of the playground and other social areas in the school that she has taken.

Questions for consideration:

1   Who will Emma have to obtain consent from to conduct her research ethically? How will Emma ensure that the participants understand the research and are giving voluntary consent?
2   How should Emma approach the transect walks? How can Emma plan the walks so that the participants feel comfortable?

(Continued)

3   How should Emma approach the research conversations? What should her role be during the conversations?
4   Are there any specific ethical considerations with regard to the images of the playground and social areas?
5   Are there any other ethical considerations specific to this example that Emma should take into account? (The answers are at the end of the chapter.)

Recommended reading

For those interested in reading more about (auto)ethnography, we recommend accessing the following:

- Hammersley, M. and Atkinson, P. (2019) *Ethnography: Principles in Practice*, 4th edn. London: Taylor & Francis.

Outline: This book is a useful read for those wanting to understand the methodological underpinnings and practical requirements when undertaking ethnography in the field of education. It includes many examples of prior ethnographic studies in education.

- Reed-Danahay, D. (2017) Bourdieu and critical autoethnography: Implications for research, writing, and teaching. *International Journal of Multicultural Education*, 19(1): 144–54.

Outline: This paper advocates employing the autoethnographic approach. Although the subject focus of her paper is immigration, the methodological arguments are easily translatable to an educational context.

For those interested in reading more about multisensory data-collection methods, we recommend accessing the following:

- Lewis, V., Kellett, M., Robinson, C., Fraser, S. and Ding, S. (eds) (2004) *The Reality of Research with Children and Young People*. London: Sage.

Outline: This book explores a wide range of multisensory methods, specifically with children and young people. All of the chapters explore real-life research examples, which will be helpful in contextualising some of the approaches explored in our work. Chapter 8 explores the Mosaic approach that much of our chapter was inspired by.

- Sharples, M., Davison, L., Thomas, G.V. and Rudman, P.D. (2003) Children as photographers: An analysis of children's photographic behaviour and intentions at three age levels. *Visual Communication*, 2(3): 303–30.

Outline: An interesting paper exploring the role of children in photography-based research methods. This is particularly relevant to those of you hoping to employ a data-collection method that will require children to take responsibility for the photography process.

- Punch, S. (2002) Research with children: The same or different from research with adults? *Childhood, 9*(3): 321–41.

Outline: This is an excellent paper, which explores the notion of children possessing different competencies from adults, therefore requiring adapted data-collection tools. This is an important read for anyone wishing to conduct research with children in the field of special and inclusive education.

Reflective question activity 9.1 answers

1   Emma will need to gain consent from the headteacher as gatekeeper of the school, the participants' parents and the children themselves. The language levels of the children will need to be taken into account when gaining consent. For some children she may simply need to explain the research and the role that participants will play in it; for others she may need to use other scaffolding materials, such as images or written tools to ensure the participants understand the research.

2   Emma should ensure that the children lead the transect walks as far as possible. She will need to think carefully about the other children and staff members who are likely to be around during the time of her planned walks. She may consider doing them during lesson time so that children feel more comfortable to speak and move freely around a quieter school.

3   Ideally, Emma should take a relatively passive role during the research conversations, again allowing the participants to lead. She should try to conduct them in a place where participants feel comfortable to encourage maximum participation.

4   Emma needs to think carefully about avoiding taking pictures that display any looked after or other vulnerable children, as well as those who have not consented to take part in the research. Ideally, Emma should take the images of the places without other children present in them. Emma should also draw on her non-participant observation data to avoid presenting children with any images of places that may trigger unease or upset and ensure that all images prompt full participation in the research conversations.

5   Emma should seek to understand as much about the participants as possible, within the bounds of confidentiality and the school's policies. In particular, the children's diagnoses of ASD may mean that methods should be adapted further to meet their individual needs, as social interaction can become problematic for children with ASD if not planned effectively. This will ensure she is designing methods that the children will feel comfortable to participate with.

10

MANAGING, ANALYSING AND PRESENTING DATA

━━━━━━━━━━ **Chapter objectives** ━━━━━━━━━━

By the end of this chapter you will:

- ✓ Have explored important considerations with regard to managing, analysing and presenting the data you will gather within your study
- ✓ Understand some common challenges to appropriate data analysis in special and inclusive education
- ✓ Know the key features of a range of appropriate approaches to analysis of the data gathered in your study
- ✓ Have explored effective ways of communicating your findings to others

Introduction

By this stage in your reading you should have a clear plan for your research aims and questions, as well as a proposed methodological approach and data-collection tools for your study. The focus of this chapter is to support you with how to manage, analyse and present the data that you will gather. It is very common for those studying at both under-graduate and postgraduate level to become overwhelmed at the prospect of organising and analysing the often vast amounts of data that may have been gathered. However, if you plan your management and analysis process beforehand, it can be a very enjoyable experience. This is the stage at which you experience the emergence of your findings and conclusions to your study. It is where you begin to see that all of your hard work is paying off!

There is a lot to think about when planning how to manage, analyse and pres-ent your data. It will not be possible to cover all potential approaches within this chapter, nor will it be possible to explore each technique highlighted in great depth. Therefore, we urge you to access the Recommended reading at the end of this chapter before you move forward with your research. We have chosen to weight this chapter strongly in favour of managing, analysing and presenting qualitative data, rather than quantitative, as this reflects the balance of the methodology we have previously explored. However, we will highlight ways in which to manage, analyse and present quantitative data in relation to questionnaires and surveys.

Before we begin to explore managing, analysing and presenting data in greater depth, it is helpful for you to reflect upon the 'questions for consideration' below so that you have given some thought to common challenges at this stage of your research. The infor-mation we share with you in the remainder of this chapter will support you to answer these questions successfully.

Questions for consideration

Managing your data

- How will you ensure that the amount of data you will analyse is manageable?
- How will you store your data so that it is accessible when you come to analyse it?
- How will you ensure that your data is stored ethically?

Analysing your data

- Which analysis approaches are appropriate for the type of data you have gathered?
- How will you know when you have reached saturation point in your analysis?
- How will you minimise any personal bias that you may bring to the analysis process?

Presenting your data

- How will you ensure that your data presentation is appropriate for the intended audience of your write-up?
- How will you ensure that your write-up is engaging and accessible for the reader?

Managing your data

There are three important considerations that should drive your decision-making in relation to data management. These relate to:

- Ethics
- Accessibility
- The use of computer-aided qualitative data analysis software (CAQDAS)

It is important to remember that the ethical considerations explored in Chapter 4 do not end once you have gathered your data. You must continue, for example, to protect the anonymity of participants in the way that you store your data. This means you should carefully consider file names, password access and safe storage of non-digitalised data to protect participants' identities. We recommend that you access BERA's (2018) *Ethical Guidelines for Educational Research* for more information on ethical storage and management of data. BERA does note some important potential exceptions to the protection of participants' anonymity and privacy; for example, if you have undertaken an autoethnographic study (a study in which you are the sole participant, as explored in Chapter 9), or a very small-scale study in which it is not possible to protect the anonymity of the participants due to its distinguishing features. You should discuss all concerns in relation to storage of your data with your supervisor to ensure you are keeping ethical considerations in mind throughout the research process.

The considerations in relation to accessibility and the use of software or manual storage are interconnected. The accessibility of your data is paramount at this stage of your research; you need to be able to swiftly access the data you will gather once they are stored. Additionally, it is important to consider how manageable the volume of data you have stored are. You will soon begin to analyse the data you have collected, which can be a time-consuming process. You need to ensure that the amount of data you have is both manageable and accessible in the time you have available for analysis and optimally relevant in answering your research questions. At this stage, it can be helpful to weed out any data that you know are not relevant to your research aims. However, make sure that you do not confuse irrelevance with anomalies; data that are likely to yield different findings to the majority may still be highly relevant, but data that do not relate to your research questions and aims are unlikely to have relevance.

The use of computer-aided qualitative data analysis software (CAQDAS) to aid both the storage and analysis of data is prominent in our field and is therefore worth your consideration. Two of the most popular software programs are *Atlas.Ti* and *NVivo*, although there are many others that have been developed to support the management and analysis of qualitative data. Both aim to support researchers with their data storage by collating data gathered into one program, which can easily be manipulated to support accessibility. CAQDAS programs also aim to support the data analysis process by providing a range of analytic functions, which include data searching, categorising, annotation, concept mapping, hyperlinking and graph-making.

The suitability of CAQDAS for your study depends upon a range of factors, not least the nature of the data you have gathered. CAQDAS is generally aimed at supporting researchers who have gathered data that takes a narrative format, for example interview transcripts or observation notes. Therefore, its use in storing and analysing data resulting from some of the more innovative, image-based data-collection methods that were presented in Chapter 9 may not be appropriate. It is most appropriate when researchers have gathered a large amount of data from a study, which may take too long or be too difficult to analyse manually. Table 10.1 explores some positives and drawbacks of using CAQDAS in our field; it can support you when choosing between manual storage and analysis, or the use of CAQDAS.

Table 10.1 CAQDAS for data storage and analysis

Positives of CAQDAS	Drawbacks of CAQDAS
• The range of functionality offered by most CAQDAS cannot be matched by individual researchers • Large amounts of data can be stored safely, with good accessibility to support swift analysis when compared with manual analysis • Common themes can emerge quickly via digital searches on keywords • Many CAQDAS provide effective ways of presenting data/findings, via maps, graphs, tables, etc. • CAQDAS can improve researcher objectivity, but only if utilised effectively • Multiple researchers, on a given project, can collaborate to store and analyse data effectively via CAQDAS	• CAQDAS cannot analyse data by themselves; nothing can replace reflexive analysis by the researcher • CAQDAS are only effective if the researcher is able to utilise their storage and analysis functions successfully • Some researchers find that it can be more difficult to immerse themselves in the data and therefore see the linkages between data sets when they are stored digitally • Anomalies can be more difficult to identify and understand when conducting digital searches on key words as opposed to manual immersion in the data • There is often a cost involved in downloading the necessary software

Checkpoint 10.1

- Data should always be managed ethically; protecting participants' anonymity is particularly important in most studies.
- Your data should be stored so that they are easily accessible when you come to begin your analysis.
- You need to decide whether or not the use of CAQDAS is appropriate for your study, with regard to both storing and analysing the data you will have gathered.

Analysing your data

Analysing your data is an exciting process; you are entering the phase where the hours spent planning and executing your study are about to pay off, in the form of findings and conclusions. It is at this point where it is all too easy to begin to run out of steam. Many students worry that all the hours they have put into their research aren't yet yielding results and the amount of data they have gathered can seem overwhelming. Try to push through these worries; the analysis process is often the most enjoyable because you can quickly begin to see the hidden meanings in your data and the value in what you have achieved with your research. You may find that you enter into the data analysis process already having identified some themes in your data; you have likely been conducting informal analysis of them during the data-collection process.

This section on analysis is split into three areas of focus – techniques and approaches in relation to the analysis of data that are:

- *Qualitative*: Word-focused
- *Visual*: Image-focused
- *Quantitative*: Number-focused

Qualitative data analysis

You will need to undertake qualitative analysis of the data you have gathered if you have employed any of the techniques we explored in Chapters 7 to 9 that focus on words, either written or spoken. For example, if you have undertaken audio-recorded interviews or research conversations with participants, you will need to analyse the transcripts that resulted from those data-collection methods. There are a large number of approaches and techniques that can be employed to analyse qualitative data. We are only able to highlight a few in our work. However, in your wider reading, you should find that most approaches to qualitative data analysis follow a similar process. We have outlined this process in Figure 10.1, which frames our discussion for the remainder of this section. Note that Figure 10.1 is framed by reflexivity, a vital feature that permeates the entire analysis process.

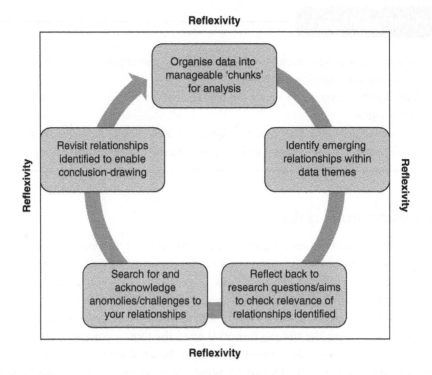

Reflexivity

Organise data into managable 'chunks' for analysis

Revisit relationships identified to enable conclusion-drawing

Identify emerging relationships within data themes

Search for and acknowledge anomolies/challenges to your relationships

Reflect back to research questions/aims to check relevance of relationships identified

Reflexivity

Reflexivity

Reflexivity

Figure 10.1   Typical features of qualitative data analysis

As can be seen from Figure 10.1, the initial aim of the analysis process is to distil your data to manageable 'chunks' for analysis, continually revisiting them to enable findings to emerge in relation to your research questions and aims. Effective analysis should always be somewhat organic in nature; if you have selected the most appropriate analysis technique(s) for your research you should find that themes emerge naturally as you continually revisit your data. A universal feature of analysing research data is that of 'coding'. Simply put, this involves identifying the main themes held within your data. You may decide to impose codes onto the data yourself and see what themes emerge or allow the codes to emerge from the data organically without imposing them at the start of the analysis process.

There are a large number of approaches that you could use to code qualitative data. We have chosen to explore some of the most common approaches used by our students in this chapter. Your selection of the most appropriate analysis technique depends on a variety of factors, including the volume of data you have gathered, time management considerations, preference with regard to using computer assistive software and the format of the data you have gathered. The approaches that we have chosen to explore include thematic coding, grounded theory and (critical) discourse analysis.

Thematic coding

Many of the terms used to describe analysis approaches in relation to qualitative data are likely to have their basis in thematic coding. At its most basic level, thematic coding involves the imposition of 'codes' onto the data you have gathered to identify relevant themes that emerge in relation to your research questions and aims. Many students choose to use their research questions as their codes. This way relevance is maintained and ensured throughout the analysis process. It is all too easy to follow an emerging thread of interest when coding your data to later find that you have spent hours collating data in relation to a theme that does not directly relate to your research questions. Placing your research questions at the heart of your analysis process avoids too many irrelevant themes emerging. Practically, undertaking a manual approach to analysis involves having your research questions (or key words from them) in front of you when going through your narrative data and colour-coding them according to theme. If using CAQDAS, you may choose to search the data using key words from your research questions and then organise the data that are selected into different files and documents for further analysis.

One example of a specific technique within thematic coding is that of the constant comparative method. Originally developed by Glaser (1965), this approach involves identifying themes and drawing conclusions from the data by both coding and analysing at the same time. The researcher 'combines systematic data collection, coding, and analysis with theoretical sampling in order to generate theory that is integrated, close to the data, and expressed in a form clear enough for further testing' (Scott et al., 1993: 280). The case study below should help you to conceptualise the practical implementation of a thematic coding approach within your study.

Case study 10.1

Thematic coding

Frieda, a PhD student in special and inclusive education, made use of the constant comparative method to analyse the interview transcripts that she gathered from one strand of her data-collection process. Frieda undertook an action research approach to explore parental engagement across three special schools in England. Although Frieda had a large amount of data to analyse (15 interview transcripts) she decided not to use CAQDAS for her analysis and, instead, preferred to analyse the data she gathered manually so that she could immerse herself more easily in the data. She did, however, make use of CAQDAS to store her data effectively.

Frieda used her research questions to scaffold her analysis. She used two different colours to mark sections of her interview transcripts that pertained to either one of her two research questions. A snapshot of her coding is provided below:

(Continued)

Research questions:

1   What are teachers' views on how successful parental engagement is in this school? (coded in italics)
2   What are teachers' views on the functionality of the 'parent views' app that is used to support parental engagement? (coded in bold)

Transcript: Teacher 1

Frieda: Can you describe the level of parental engagement that you experience in this school?

Teacher 1:   *I would say that it is mixed. We have a lot of parents who will share a lot of information about how their child is getting on at home during drop off and pick up time, but then won't want to physically come across the school boundaries to attend engagement events. Then there are the other parents who it is really hard to engage because they don't physically bring them into school, you know, they get buses or taxis in so it's harder to form that relationship with the parents. Then of course there are parents who will come to anything and everything in school and like to play a big part in the school community.* We are very proud of our school and our wider community here, you know, I don't live in the local area like many of the teachers here and lots of our children don't live close by either but their parents have chosen to send them here because they think we will do the best for them and we really do try our hardest for every single child here. **Actually, we have found that the app we're using has really targeted engagement from those parents who are happy to talk at drop off and pick up time but not at in school events because they're, erm, happy to add things digitally and without that face to face contact I think…it's hard to know what the motivation is but we have definitely noticed a better pick up from the parents who didn't like coming into school much but now will share and comment on things via the app.**

Once Frieda had fully coded her data, she then organised all coded sections of the same colour into distinct documents and revisited those sections to identify commonality, and differences, between participants' responses. By continually revisiting her data, Frieda was able to maintain reflexivity throughout her analysis process and successfully identified a range of themes that she was able to compare with prior research and make recommendations for practice and further research.

Grounded theory

Loosely linked to the constant comparative approach to the coding of qualitative data, another technique of analysis is that of grounded theory. At a basic level, the grounded theory approach involves entering into the analysis process without predetermined codes for your analysis. So, unlike standardised thematic coding in which you may choose your research aims and questions to scaffold your analysis process, with grounded theory you let the codes emerge from the data organically. You are able to follow in the directions that the data lead you. With this approach it is particularly important to ensure that your analysis process stays directly relevant to your research questions and aims; the unstructured nature of this approach can make this challenging. As with the constant comparative approach, continually revisiting your data is important in order to reach saturation point (the point at which you are confident that no new themes are emerging when you revisit the data).

Confusingly, the grounded theory approach is used by some to describe their entire methodological approach, not only their approach to data analysis (refer back to Chapter 6 for the distinction between these two). Grounded theory, as a methodological approach, is often most appropriate when students are intending to focus their research on a relatively new or under-researched area. In this case, a minimal number of prior publications can mean that there are few existing codes that can be used to scaffold the analysis of data; instead, the grounded theory approach provides a mechanism for a range of themes to emerge without being constrained by a minimal number of findings from previous research. When used solely during the data analysis process, grounded theory can be very appropriate if the context of the research is quite different from that of prior research in your area of interest. The organic nature of the grounded theory approach can be its real strength; it acknowledges the uniqueness of much research in special and inclusive educational contexts.

(Critical) discourse analysis

Another popular approach to analysing qualitative data is that of (critical) discourse analysis. The word 'discourse' is used to mean data that are comprised of the spoken and written word, so you can think of it as data that have been gathered through methods that involve talking or writing. This data may have been gathered through interviews, diary entries, ethnographic observations or other narrative-focused methods. As with grounded theory, critical discourse analysis is used by some to describe their entire methodological approach, not only their approach to data analysis. However, for the purposes of this chapter we have chosen to explore it simply as a tool for data analysis.

The difference between standardised discourse analysis and that of critical discourse analysis can be thought of using a layered analogy. In this first layer, you analyse your discourse-related data to identify key themes within what the participants have said or written, much as you would with thematic coding. However, when conducting *critical* discourse analysis, the focus is on moving a step further than simple coding of the data for key themes and attempting to analyse the meaning behind the discourse. The reason for exploring the meaning behind the language people use has its origins in philosophical debate. Foucault viewed discourse as an instrument and an effect of power (Danaher et al., 2000). It reflects an individual's ideology and is shaped by the environment and experiences of an individual, and can therefore yield fascinating insights into the context in which your research is situated. As much research in the field of education takes place in, and is strongly linked to, unique schools or other educational institutions, critical discourse analysis can be a highly relevant data analysis approach within special and inclusive education.

Case study 10.2

Critical discourse analysis

Maria, an MA student in special and inclusive education, was interested in exploring primary school-aged (7–11) physically disabled students' attitudes towards the staff members they interacted with regularly. She wanted to identify any power differentials, as perceived by the students, between the teachers, teaching assistants (TAs) and learning mentors in the school.

Extract from research conversation with one participant:

Researcher: Can you tell me about Miss M (Learning Mentor)?

Participant: She's just like a part-teacher. She helps us learn to move around her kitchen that she has in her office and we have breakfast there a lot. She doesn't do any proper work with us like Mrs F (Teacher) and Mr G (TA)…really we just have fun with her. It's like we can go to her when we have any problems or don't want to play outside at lunch time and she'll just let us have fun in her office when we can't do the work.

Initial discourse analysis

If Maria were to undertake standardised discourse analysis on this extract, she might highlight that the student clearly perceives a difference in the roles of the three staff members she identifies. She may highlight that the student perceives the role of the learning mentor as aligned with non-academic tasks and only links the roles of the teacher and TA with learning.

Critical discourse analysis

As Maria moved a layer deeper and conducted critical discourse analysis on this extract, she highlighted that the use of the words 'just,' 'part-teacher' and 'doesn't do any proper work' indicate that there is a perceived power differential between the role of the learning mentor and that of the TA and teacher; the student clearly regards the latter as occupying higher-status roles. Additionally, the use of the phrase 'let us have fun' indicates that the student may not naturally liken the notion of school to fun, as they may believe 'fun' has to be sanctioned or enabled by the staff, rather than being an integral part of the learning experience.

Analysis of imagery

Some of the multisensory data-collection methods that we recommended in Chapter 9 will result in image-focused data – for example, photographs, comic strips or drawings. If you are hoping to employ one of these methods in your research, it is important that you know how to analyse the resulting images effectively. It is often said that 'a picture speaks a thousand words'. The richness of the data contained within a single image can therefore provide you with a lot to analyse and a range of themes to distil into findings. As with word-based qualitative data there are a range of approaches to analysing imagery successfully. We have chosen to focus upon interpretive phenomenological analysis (IPA) in this chapter, as we believe it is often the most appropriate approach to analysis in our field as it takes account of the uniqueness of many contexts in special and inclusive education.

The IPA approach to the analysis of imagery is one that centres primarily on understanding an individual's view of their context or the phenomenon of interest; only then is the researcher able to interpret the images that have been produced and explored together effectively. Some researchers believe that the fullness of an individual's lived experiences are not easy to understand through analysis of verbal data alone. Imagery can therefore be used to encourage participants to share hard-to-reach aspects of their lived experiences (Boden et al., 2019). Similar to the approach followed in critical discourse analysis, the IPA approach requires you to move past the image itself and understand the hidden meanings behind it. The case study below should give you a sense of how IPA can be used in practice.

Case study 10.3

Analysis of drawings

Leona, a PhD student in inclusive pedagogy, focused her research on the development of friendships between primary-aged students with an identified special educational need and those who were not identified with additional needs. She was interested in exploring the dynamics within these relationships and hoped to identify the roles that each student played within their friendships. Leona used multisensory data-collection methods; she asked each participant to draw images of themselves and their friends, using research conversations to scaffold discussion around the images produced. Leona used IPA to analyse the drawings produced by the students. An example of her early analysis of one drawing is shown in Figure 10.2.

(Continued)

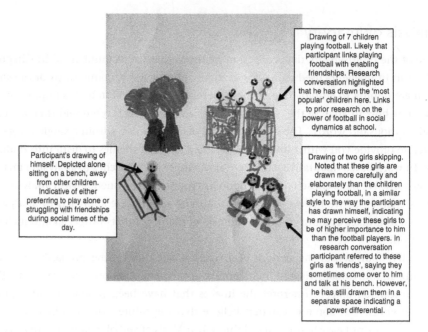

Figure 10.2 Analysis of child's drawing

Checkpoint 10.2

- Most analysis of qualitative data involves the identification of themes via 'coding'.
- You will need to decide whether or not software programs are appropriate for use with your process of analysis.
- You may wish to impose some codes onto your data at the beginning of the process of analysis to identify findings that are directly relevant to your research aims; for example, via thematic coding.
- You may wish to allow the codes to emerge from the data organically – for example via the grounded theory approach.
- In order to analyse images successfully, you need to look for 'hidden meanings' by considering the context of your participants.
- It is important to analyse images alongside the other data you have gathered to fully appreciate their significance and enable a better understanding to be drawn from them.

Activity 10.1

Analysing imagery

Choose an image that you're interested in analysing. It doesn't need to be an image related to your proposed research topic; you can choose anything that interests you. Try to answer some of the questions below to help you scaffold your analysis. Remember that if you are analysing images as part of your study, you must ensure that the questions you ask yourself during the analysis process are directly relevant to enabling you to answer your research questions and meet your research aims.

- Do you know who created the image? For what purpose?
- What or who was the intended audience for the image?
- Can you describe the features of the image (colours, style, composition, features, etc.)?
- Are there any particularly striking features of the image? If so, what makes them striking?
- Are there any people in the image? If so, what does the image convey about them?
- Can you identify anything about the context behind the image?
- Do you think there are any political or socio-cultural messages conveyed by the image? If so, what do you think the intended messages are?
- Can you identify any conflicting interpretations of the image?
- From what perspective are you analysing this image? Can you identify any personal biases that may heavily influence your interpretation of the image?

Quantitative data analysis

The techniques that we have focused on so far within this chapter have related exclusively to the analysis of qualitative data. However, some of you may decide to collect quantitative data. For example, within a case study methodology you may decide to collect data using questionnaires. Others may need to analyse specific numerical data sets that are relevant to your research aims – for example, academic grading data or open-access school performance data produced by government departments. As with the analysis of qualitative data, it is important to consider the role of data analysis software when planning your approach. It is highly likely that you will need to use software to support your analysis if you are dealing with large data sets. The only exception is if you have a small number of paper-copy questionnaires, which can be easily analysed manually. Nevertheless, we would always recommend using a program that can store and undertake basic analysis of quantitative data if you have gathered them; Microsoft Excel can be a good place to begin. For larger amounts of quantitative data, you are likely to benefit from a more advanced program, such as Statistical Package for the Social Sciences (SPSS), which is the most widely used program of this type in the social sciences.

To use SPSS to aid your analysis, you will need to familiarise yourself with its functions, which we cannot go into detail about here. If you are thinking of using this in your study, please refer to the Recommended reading at the end of this chapter. To give you a sense of the functionality of SPSS, you can use it to create distinct databases of data you have gathered. These databases can be viewed in different ways, according to different variables; for example, in a questionnaire about students' views on the inclusivity of their setting you may choose a label for each variable denoted by each separate question that was asked. It is the ability of SPSS to sort and analyse data via variables that distinguishes it from Excel; because it works with databases, it is able to hold lots of useful information about your variables that Excel is not able to. You can use SPSS to manipulate data in many different ways – for example, finding means, medians and modes in your data as well as other frequency functions. One of the most important and most useful functions of programs like SPSS, and indeed CAQDAS programs more generally, is their ability to produce visual representations of your analysis – for example, via tables, graphs and diagrams.

Presenting data

You may now have an appropriate plan for the analysis of all the data you have gathered in your study – well done! You must now give some thought to the most appropriate ways of presenting the data you have gathered, the findings you have identified and the conclusions that you have drawn. The most important consideration at this stage of your research is your intended audience. You need to think about who you are writing for and which mediums will be most successful in conveying your findings to them. It is likely that your primary audience will be your supervisor and the markers of your finished thesis. These people are likely to be specialists in your field of research; however, it is important not to assume that they understand the complexity of your research as you do. Additionally, some of you may be hoping to publish aspects of your research in the future; if so, you need to consider how accessible it is to a non-specialist in your field. It is vital that you define any complex terms for the reader and avoid overly complex language in your write-up. One of most important phrases we use with our students to support their data presentation is that you must 'lead the reader through your writing'. You are taking them on a journey through your research; try to keep them with you at all times and avoid losing them to complex sentence structure or lack of explanation. You will learn more about how to ensure your writing is appropriate for your audience in Chapter 11.

By far the most common approach to presenting data in our field is through the use of text. However, you should consider interspersing your written work with some visual tools of data presentation. Many students make good use of graphs, tables and diagrams to highlight relationships and patterns within their data. This is an excellent way of supporting the reader to identify clearly the source of the findings that you have presented in your data. Additionally, some of the multisensory data-collection methods explored in Chapter 9 provide you with further interesting ways to visually present your data. If you have included methods that involve photographs, comic strips or drawings, you should try to include examples in your write-up so that the reader can see clearly how and from what you have drawn your conclusions. Some of the most successful data presentation and analysis chapters are those in which researchers have created their own diagrams or tables to highlight the patterns in the data that they have identified.

Checkpoint 10.3

- When analysing quantitative data, we urge you to strongly consider the use of appropriate software to support your analysis, for example SPSS.
- When presenting data of all forms, consider using a range of visual mediums to support the reader in navigating your key findings, for example graphs, figures, tables, diagrams and images.
- Your focus at all times during your write-up should be on 'leading the reader through your writing'.

Chapter summary

At this point, it may be useful for you to reflect on the questions for consideration that were presented at the beginning of this chapter to ensure that you are confident to answer them and ready to begin the process of analysis. A final consideration to leave you with in this chapter relates to evidencing your work. You should now be familiar with a range of ways of analysing the data you have gathered in your study and then how to present your data and findings using a range of mediums. However, there is one final step that you must not overlook. Once your findings are clear, you need to consider how they compare to previous research. To do this, you should refer back to the literature that you will have reviewed to inform your research questions and aims, right at the start of the research process, and let the reader know how your findings compare. If you do this then you are likely to be able to produce robust, reliable and valid conclusions from your study. Refer back to the information shared in Chapter 5 to support you with this process.

Recommended reading

One of the most useful ways of researching different data analysis and presentation techniques in our field is to access free online e-theses libraries to find examples of previous studies that have made use of the approaches that you are interested in. Perhaps starting with your own university would be sensible.

If you are interested in reading more about qualitative data analysis, we recommend the following:

- Merriam, S.B. and Tisdell, E.J. (2015) *Qualitative Research: A Guide to Design and Implementation*, 4th edn. San Francisco, CA: Jossey-Bass.

Outline: Chapter 8 of this book gives a clear, uncomplicated description about how to approach the process of 'coding' and is a useful first text to explore when beginning to plan your approach to analysis.

- Rogers, R. (ed.) (2011) *An Introduction to Critical Discourse Analysis in Education*. London: Routledge.

Outline: A comprehensive text that outlines key debates and approaches to critical discourse analysis in the field of education specifically.

- Jackson, K. and Bazeley, P. (2019) *Qualitative Data Analysis with NVivo*. London: Sage.

Outline: A good text for those of you interested in using CAQDAS in your analysis of qualitative data.

We would also recommend Boden et al. (2019) for those of you looking to utilise interpretive phenomenological analysis (IPA) to analyse image-focused data.

If you are interested in reading more about quantitative data analysis, we recommend the following:

- Hinton, P.R., McMurray, I. and Brownlow, C. (2014) *SPSS Explained*. London: Routledge.

Outline: A comprehensive, easy-to-follow, step-by-step text that supports you to understand the functionality and usability of SPSS in quantitative data analysis.

11

MOVING FORWARD

═══════ **Chapter objectives** ═══════

By the end of this chapter you will:

✓ Have explored appropriate ways to scaffold the write-up of your study
✓ Understand how to adapt your writing to a range of audiences
✓ Have reflected upon the successes and areas for improvement in your study
✓ Know potential avenues for exploration beyond your study, relating to potential improvements in practice and publication

Introduction

Throughout this book we have aimed to support you with the whole process of conducting successful research in the field of special and inclusive education. As you approach this final chapter, your research process should be near completion. You will have collected and analysed all of your data and your findings should have emerged. In this chapter we turn our attention to the final phase of the research process, the writing up. This chapter explores a range of considerations relating to writing up and maximising the outcomes of the research you have carefully conducted. The decisions that you make at this final stage can be the difference between a passable piece of work and a publishable piece of work, so ensure that you give the areas explored in this chapter your full consideration.

Scaffolding your write-up

The final stage of writing up is often not as daunting as it may initially seem once you get going; you will already have the majority of your chapters drafted before you come to your final write-up. If you have followed the format of this book then you should already have drafts of your research questions and methodology, review of the literature in your chosen area of interest, as well as your data presentation and analysis. This final stage is more about formatting your writing so that it creates a coherent whole (a dissertation or thesis), rather than starting from scratch. Depending upon which research approach you have taken (see Chapter 6 for a reminder of common methodological approaches in special and inclusive education), your dissertation or thesis should follow a clear format, regardless of the level at which you are studying. The most common format is shared in Figure 11.1 and is indicative of the studies that have followed an empirical methodological approach (those who have undertaken data collection in the field).

The format shared in Figure 11.1 should be viewed as an example only; studies vary significantly, and you should spend some time considering how to structure your chapters so that they share your work most effectively. If you are studying at undergraduate level, your word limit might prevent you exploring all of the suggested areas of focus shared in Figure 11.1. Equally, if you are studying at PhD level then you are likely to require additional chapters to share all of your work. Often, students at PhD level opt to include multiple literature review and data presentation and analysis chapters, as this approach can better aid presentation of the large amount of literature/data that they have analysed. Using the research questions for a given study as chapter titles can be an excellent way of systematically exploring both the literature and data gathered.

If you have chosen to use a non-empirical methodological approach in your study (see Chapter 6 for a reminder of this), the 'desk-based' nature of your study means that the traditional thesis structure outlined in Figure 11.1 is likely to be less suitable for you. As you have not gathered data out in the field, a traditional literature review (followed

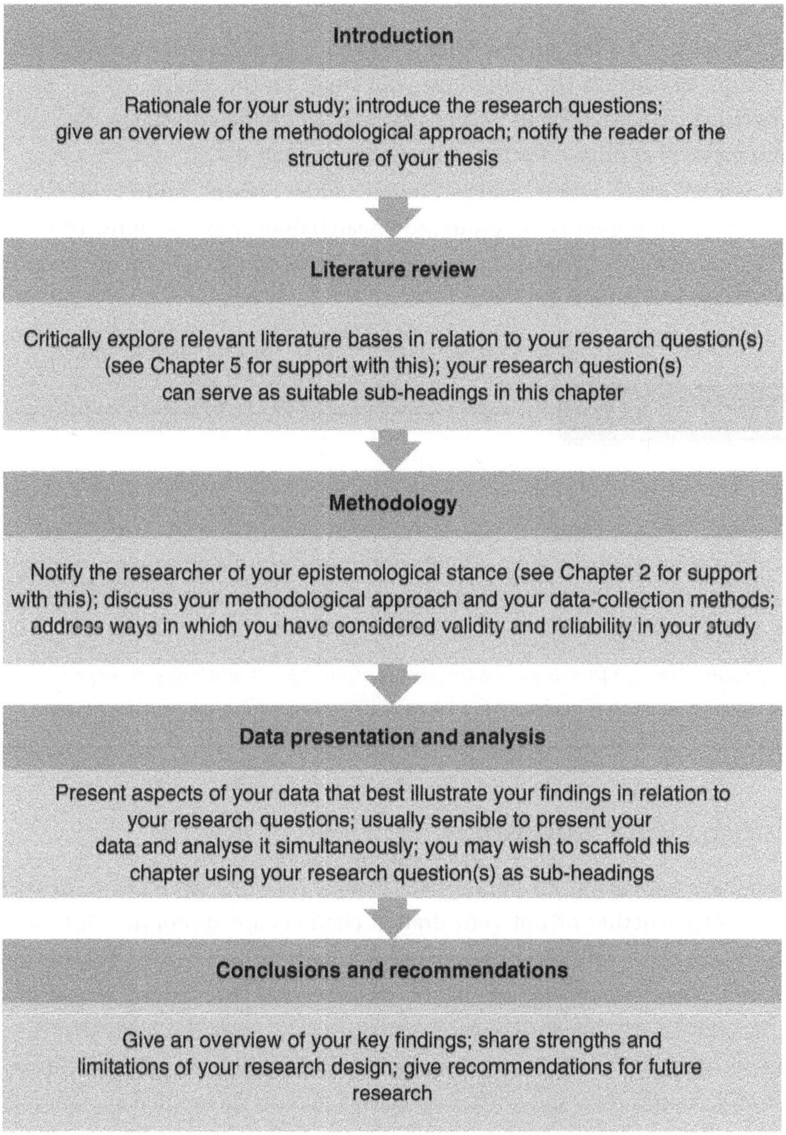

Introduction

Rationale for your study; introduce the research questions; give an overview of the methodological approach; notify the reader of the structure of your thesis

Literature review

Critically explore relevant literature bases in relation to your research question(s) (see Chapter 5 for support with this); your research question(s) can serve as suitable sub-headings in this chapter

Methodology

Notify the researcher of your epistemological stance (see Chapter 2 for support with this); discuss your methodological approach and your data-collection methods; address ways in which you have considered validity and reliability in your study

Data presentation and analysis

Present aspects of your data that best illustrate your findings in relation to your research questions; usually sensible to present your data and analyse it simultaneously; you may wish to scaffold this chapter using your research question(s) as sub-headings

Conclusions and recommendations

Give an overview of your key findings; share strengths and limitations of your research design; give recommendations for future research

Figure 11.1 Common format when writing up empirical studies

by methodology and then data presentation and analysis) is unlikely to fit the format of your research. You will need to think carefully about ways in which to lead the reader through your writing so that your finished thesis or dissertation hangs together as a cohesive whole but is divided into manageable sections. Many of our students find that a variation of the structure below is better suited to sharing their studies effectively, particularly if following a systematic literature review methodological approach:

- *Introduction*
- *Initial scoping of the literature*: Highlight key themes in the core literature related to your topic of interest; this will frame your study for the reader
- *Methodology*: This is likely to be a relatively short chapter outlining the non-empirical approach to data collection and analysis
- *Literature review/discussion chapters*: Students often present multiple literature review chapters, often presented according to research questions and aims. These chapters will simultaneously present and analyse the secondary data sources referred to
- *Conclusions and recommendations*

Checkpoint 11.1

- You will need to spend time considering ways in which to structure your dissertation or thesis; explore prior students' write-ups for inspiration.
- Your final write-up should involve re-drafting rather than starting from scratch; you should already have most of your chapters in draft form when you come to assemble your thesis or dissertation.
- Remember that the primary consideration should be on leading the reader through your writing. It must therefore be presented in manageable sections throughout.

Writing to your audience

Once you have settled on an appropriate format for your dissertation or thesis, you should consider whether or not your drafted chapters are appropriate for the inended audience. Ideally, you will have considered this early in the writing process but if you haven't, don't despair. Now is your chance to ensure that your writing is as clear as possible to your audience. If you are a research student at any level, it is likely that the primary audience for your work will be your supervisor and other academics within your field from within your university and further afield. Therefore, as we touched upon in Chapter 10, it is important that your writing takes account of their background. This is often a daunting task for students, who feel pressure to write 'academically'; we will explore what this means in practice in the rest of this section.

Take a few minutes to imagine that you are writing up your research for a newspaper. It may be helpful to pick up a local newspaper and explore the ways in which research findings have been reported by journalists. Consider the language used and other tools used to maintain the reader's interest. You are likely to see a range of emotive language and sensationalised findings; newspapers need to capture a reader's interest early on by using language that stirs emotion and encourages you to read further into the article. You may also discover that little attention is paid to the methodology or evidence base for the findings; there is a perception that readers are often less interested in the way in which findings have been gathered and more interested in the findings themselves. Exploring news articles is a very helpful way to highlight writing approaches that link to specific audiences. It will give you confidence that you already know many approaches to avoid when writing up your research! Of course, newspaper articles are very obviously different from academic literature, but exploring a variety of different publication types is always helpful in supporting you with what to avoid and what to employ in your writing style.

The most useful publication types to consult when developing your own writing style include journal articles, books, e-theses and dissertations. During your extensive reading for your study, you are likely to have noticed that some journal articles appear to be more accessible and digestible, whereas others can be too complex and difficult to navigate. It is helpful to go back to those at both ends of the reading spectrum and note down aspects of the writing styles used by different authors so that you can identify tools to make your own writing more accessible to your audience. Similarly, many universities have comprehensive repositories for past e-theses and dissertations at a range of levels of study, which you can search to identify those that may be useful to you in your write-up. These past studies can help with layout and formatting approaches, literature suggestions, as well as more general stylistic ideas and tools for you to consider using in your own writing. It is always a good idea to go to the repository of the university you are studying with first, but some of the most helpful links to open access online repositories for our students have been:

- The British Library's online PhD e-theses repository, which holds records of most of the PhD theses submitted in the UK, the majority of which are downloadable (https://ethos.bl.uk/Home.do)
- PhD/MA e-theses at the University of Birmingham (https://etheses.bham.ac.uk)
- PhD e-theses via the White Rose network (combined repository for the Universities of York, Leeds and Sheffield) (https://etheses.whiterose.ac.uk)

Once you have consulted a range of other literature, you are likely to find that writing academically may not look as you had initially expected. It is a common pitfall for students to think that academic writing involves using lots of big words, long sentences and complex terminology. In fact, we would argue that it is often the opposite. Good academic writing should be clear and easy to read, avoiding overly complex terminology and long sentences. Remember that you need to lead the reader through your writing. Your markers may have another few theses to mark in the week that they mark yours; they don't want to have to wade through endless paragraphs of complex sentence structure to find your argument! Be clear and succinct and your writing is more likely to be better understood by your audience.

Concluding your study

When you are happy with the way you have presented the findings to emerge from your study, you'll need to spend some time considering how to approach your conclusion. This is often a section that students can rush through too quickly, eager to finish the process.

However, a good conclusion is important; you need to leave the reader with a positive impression of the quality of your writing in order to ensure your marks reflect the quality of your work.

Your concluding chapter can be a very satisfying chapter to write. Your other chapters are likely to have been tightly constrained by very specific subheadings, which can leave you minimal flexibility. However, you have more scope here to focus your discussion on the areas that you decide are most worthy of consideration.

It is very important that you don't use your conclusion to simply summarise the findings of your research. Although you may have a subsection that briefly highlights your main findings, the substantive part of this chapter should cover reflections on the research process, highlighting what your research means for the wider special and inclusive education community and identifying opportunities for wider research and implications for policy.

One of the largest sections within your concluding chapter is likely to be a reflection upon the successes and areas for improvement within the study you have conducted. Remember that effective criticality involves acknowledging the things that didn't quite go as planned or weren't quite appropriate in meeting your research aims. Acknowledging the flaws in your research can highlight your ability to be critical, which is always positive. If you have planned and executed your study carefully then you should never be in a position where the methodology did not allow your research aims to be met, so don't worry too much about acknowledging the flaws that you identify; they should never render your research invalid. The case study below highlights an appropriate approach to both sharing the successes and acknowledging the limitations of a given study.

Case study 11.1

Extract from a concluding chapter

Amina conducted her research on the appropriateness and efficacy of resources used in secondary schools to support transgender children in an area of the South East of England. An extract from her concluding chapter is presented below. This extract highlights an effective approach to acknowledging the challenges faced in her research; she shares them openly and successfully argues the case for the approach she has taken, using literature to validate her arguments.

> One of the greatest challenges was the low availability of contexts that met the sampling criteria for this piece of research. The school sampled needed to have experience of having supported at least three children who had struggled with gender identity whilst in their care. Initial sampling was snowball in effect, as schools needed to be identified via word of mouth, due to the lack of reporting around transgender experiences in school. This could be argued to lack academic rigor, however, the specificity of this research meant that convenience sampling was imperative in order to make the research viable (Smith, 2017)...

The professional bias that the researcher brought to the research process could be argued to be both a positive and negative regarding the reliability and validity of this research. The researcher's prior experience of struggling to find effective resources to support a transgender child in her tutor group was difficult to remove from her analysis process. This professional bias may have reduced the objectivity of the researcher's findings. Yet, as argued by Fielding (2015), subjectivity is unavoidable when a professional is conducting research in a context familiar to them. Similarly, as Davis (2018) highlights, the particularisation of one case study, undertaken by one researcher, can be its richness. It provides a 'force of example,' which can be tested via future research (Flyvbjerg, 2006).

To further support you in reviewing and reflecting upon your research process, it may be useful for you to spend some time contemplating the 'questions for review' in the activity box below. You will probably not have scope to address them all in your conclusion but they should give you plenty of food for thought when exploring your successes and limitations. In general, you should direct your thinking for this section towards answering the following question: 'If you could undertake your research again, is there anything that you would do differently?'

Activity 11.1

Questions for review

Reviewing the scope of your research:

- Did your research questions/aims result in a good amount of relevant data that yielded strong findings?
- Were there any areas that you feel should/should not have been explored to make your study stronger?
- Did your study result in findings that could be deemed an original contribution to your field?
- Can you identify any areas for future research, outside of the scope of your study, that would be beneficial to your field?
- Do any of your findings have implications for current policy and practice in the area of special and inclusive education?

Reviewing your personal approach:

- Did you keep to your research timeline or did personal events change your plans?
- Did you successfully minimise your personal and professional biases, or was that more difficult once your research was underway?

(Continued)

Reviewing your methodology:

- Did all of your data collection go to plan?
- Did your planned data-collection schedule work as intended, or were there logistical barriers that you had to navigate (for example, changes in school routine or availability of staff)?
- Did your planned key word search terms result in relevant literature, or did you have to refine them once your research was underway?
- If you used software, was this appropriate in supporting you to meet your research aims?

Checkpoint 11.2

- Use examples of past e-theses to support you in determining the most appropriate structure for your write-up.
- Remember that writing academically is often characterised by clear, uncomplicated and concise sentences.
- Avoid rushing the writing of your conclusion.
- Make sure that your conclusion does more than just summarise your key findings; focus on exploring what went well and what you could have done differently.

Defending your study

If you are studying at PhD level, it is likely that you may have to undertake an oral exam, or viva, in order to defend the work that you have produced. This can be a nerve-wracking time for many students. You have spent years being in control of the direction of your research and you may feel disarmed at the thought of the final stages of the process being somewhat out of your control; the examiners control the direction of the viva and the questions that are asked. However, you need to remember that no one understands the intricacies of your research like you do. You will know the literature that you have explored inside out, and to a level that the examiners are highly unlikely to. You should enter the viva process knowing that you are the expert in relation to your research.

Some supervisors may involve you in the process of identifying an appropriate external examiner for your thesis. If this occurs and your supervisor asks you for any thoughts or recommendations as to who may be suitable, then take that opportunity. You are likely to be able to identify some academics who will appreciate the direction and approach you have taken in your research. Unfortunately, the response of different examiners to your work can be a bit of a lottery; choosing supervisors who have similar research approaches and ideologies in the area you have chosen to research can support a more meaningful process.

The general purpose of the role of examiners is to check that the approaches you have taken in your research are valid and reliable, and that your research contributes some originality to your field. It should not be an opportunity for examiners to criticise or attempt to discredit every aspect of your research. Most viva stories that we have heard are positive and have provided students with a notable sense of achievement after having successfully defended their research. However, there can be times when the examination panel may disagree on the quality and credibility of a student's work, which can be challenging to navigate for the student. However, even if the process doesn't quite go to plan, you know your research better than the examiners do; as long as you can credibly defend your decisions then you will come through and, in time, will feel better skilled because of it. It will also help you, if you end up working in academia, to understand more about how to supervise and examine PhDs in the most appropriate and professional way possible.

Beyond your study

Once you have submitted your work and successfully passed your degree or research module, you may quickly start thinking about moving forward from your research. For some of you, completing your research will be enough, but others of you may wish to publish aspects of your research. Some of you may even wish to undertake further research, based upon the recommendations of your study, or aim to pursue a career in academia. Whichever path you take, you should consider whether the study you have completed may have meaningful implications for practice in special and inclusive education. If it does, then it is worth considering ways to disseminate your findings further.

If you decide to disseminate your findings more widely, you need to consider carefully the most appropriate publication type for your work to ensure that it reaches your target audience. Similarly, as was explored earlier in this chapter, you need to ensure that your research is written to reflect your target audience. This will mean that you will need to re-draft aspects of your write-up to ensure it meets the needs of the publication(s) you write for. You are unlikely to be able to publish your study in its entirety; word limits mean that you may need to select aspects of your study to publish separately. If you have undertaken a particularly innovative approach to data collection, for example, you may wish to dedicate a paper to exploring this alone. Similarly, there may be a particularly compelling finding to emerge from your work that you think may form the basis of a research article. Think carefully about how to break your work up into 'chunks' and use them to scaffold papers for your target audience(s).

Many of you may wish to share your findings with teachers and other educational professionals in the hope that they may inform improvements to practice. If so, you may wish to explore opportunities to write for a teacher-focused magazine/blog, such as the *TES* or *Schools Week*. Or you may wish to submit an article to a practice-focused journal (which may be subject to peer review), bridging the gap between academia and practice, such as *Support for Learning*.

Those of you wishing to share your work with wider academic audiences may wish to explore submission of an article to journals focused on special and inclusive education that disseminate national/international empirical research, primarily to academics. These journals often have strict submission criteria, which must be followed if you are to have a paper accepted. They will also involve peer review, which means that the academic rigour of your research must stand up to scrutiny by other academics in your field. It is very important that you explore the suitability of your research for a given journal before submitting an expression of interest or a drafted article. Many students can fall at the first hurdle by submitting a qualitative research paper to a journal that is heavily in favour of quantitative studies, for example. Some journals that primarily seek submission on empirical research studies in special and inclusive education include:

- *Journal of Research in Special Educational Needs (JORSEN)*
- *British Journal of Special Education (BJSE)*
- *European Journal of Special Needs Education*
- *Educational Research Review*
- *International Journal of Disability, Development and Education*
- *British Journal of Learning Disabilities*
- *International Journal of Inclusive Education*

It is important to note that the rejection rate of papers submitted to peer review is very high. Do not be disheartened if your first few attempts at publication fail; take the feedback that the reviewers give you and refine your draft to support higher chances of publication. What works for one journal will not work for another, so ensure that the journal you choose is right for your paper.

Whilst you are wading through the world of peer review and publication, you may wish to explore opportunities to speak at conferences, to share your work and make connections with others in your area of interest. Many students choose to begin their conference career at the familiar university in which they have studied; this can be a good way of building your confidence in presenting. You can explore opportunities to present at teacher-focused conferences to disseminate your findings to practitioners. Or you may wish to explore opportunities to present at larger national or international research conferences to build your profile in academia. Your supervisors can often be a great help in indicating which conferences might be most suitable for you and your work.

Checkpoint 11.3

- If you need to defend your work via an oral examination, remember that you are the expert on your research; focus on justifying your decisions rather than worrying about your work being inadequate.

- When considering moving beyond your study, let the target audience drive your dissemination decisions.
- Don't be disheartened if your attempts to publish aren't successful at the beginning; use reviewers' comments to improve your next submission.

Chapter summary and final word

The research journey is very rarely straightforward, especially in the field of special and inclusive education, where research contexts can be ever-changing and adapting to support the varying needs of individuals. This book has presented you with a range of approaches that you might like to adopt for your research in special and inclusive education and has shown that there are ways to gather the opinions and share the voices of those who might be considered vulnerable. We have argued that a creative and flexible approach is needed to ensure that the views and experiences of all stakeholders in inclusive education are heard. This is especially true for those whose voices continue to remain under-represented within the research literatures. We encourage you not to shy away from finding ways to make these voices heard; we have much to learn from them and your research will be much richer for capturing them.

Finally, remember that conducting a piece of research as part of a qualification is as much about enabling you to grow as a researcher as it is about gaining the degree or passing your course or module. It is an excellent opportunity for you to dedicate some of your time to building skills and learning more about an area that really interests you; don't let the challenging times detract from enjoyment of the process overall.

Recommended reading

- Chapter 9 in Thomas, G. (2017) *How to Do Your Research Project: A Guide for Students*. London: Sage.

Outline: This chapter provides some useful complementary detail about how to conclude, writing up and present your research. We particularly recommend Table 9.1 which outlines key functions of your conclusion alongside some example phrases that you could use in your own writing.

- Thomson, P. and Kamler, B. (2013) *Writing for Peer-Reviewed Journals: Strategies for Getting Published*. London: Routledge.

Outline: This is a useful text for those wishing to publish the research they did for their thesis or dissertation in an academic journal. It covers all parts of the process, illustrating them with real student examples and case studies.

- Wyse, D. and Cowan, K. (2017) *The Good Writing Guide for Education Students*, 4th edn. London: Sage.

Outline: This book guides students through the key elements of good writing. It includes dedicated chapters on structuring your writing, writing critically, writing a dissertation, referencing and proofreading.

REFERENCES

Abbott, L. and Langston, A. (2005) Ethical research with very young children, in A. Farrell (ed.), *Ethical Research with Children*. Maidenhead: Open University Press. pp.37–48.

Ainscow, M. and Booth, T. (eds) (1998) *From Them to Us: An International Study of Inclusion in Education*. London: Routledge.

Alderson, P. (2005) Designing ethical research with children, in A. Farrell (ed.), *Ethical Research with Children*. Maidenhead: Open University Press. pp. 27–36.

Alderson, P. and Morrow, V. (2020) *The Ethics of Research with Children and Young People. A Practical Handbook*. London: Sage.

Avramidis, E. and Wilde, A. (2010) Evaluating the social impacts of inclusion through a multi-method research design. *Education 3–13*, 37(4): 323–34.

Bassey, M. (2001) A solution to the problem of generalisation in educational research: Fuzzy prediction. *Oxford Review of Education*, 27(1): 5–22.

Begley, A. (2000) The educational self-perception of children with Down syndrome, in A. Lewis and G. Lindsay (eds) *Researching Children's Perspectives*. Milton Keynes: Open University Press. pp. 98–111.

Blatchford, P., Russell, A. and Webster, R. (2012) *Reassessing the Impact of Teaching Assistants: How Research Challenges Practice and Policy*. London: Routledge.

Boden, Z., Larkin, M. and Iyer, M. (2019) Picturing ourselves in the world: Drawings, interpretative phenomenological analysis and the relational mapping interview. *Qualitative Research in Psychology*, 16(2): 218–36.

Boland, A., Cherry, G. and Dickson, R. (eds) (2017) *Doing a Systematic Review: A Student's Guide*. London: Sage.

Bourke, R., Loveridge, J., O'Neill, J., Erueti, B. and Jamieson, A. (2017) A sociocultural analysis of the ethics of involving children in educational research. *International Journal of Inclusive Education*, 21(3): 259–71.

Boxall, K. and Ralph, S. (2009) Research ethics and the use of visual images in research with people with intellectual disability. *Journal of Intellectual and Developmental Disability*, 34(1): 45–54.

Breathnach, H., Danby, S. and O'Gorman, L. (2018) Becoming a member of the classroom: Supporting children's participation as informants in research. *European Early Childhood Education Research Journal*, 26(3): 393–406.

British Educational Research Association (BERA) (2018) *Ethical Guidelines for Educational Research*, 4th edn. London: BERA. www.bera.ac.uk/publication/ethical-guidelines-for-educational-research-2018

Buckler, S. and Walliman, N. (2016) *Your Dissertation in Education*, 2nd edn. London: Sage.

Bucknall, S. (2014) Doing qualitative research with children and young people, in A. Clark, R. Flewitt, M. Hammersley and M. Robb (eds) *Understanding Research with Children and Young People*. London: Sage. pp. 69–84.

Burton, N., Brundrett, M. and Jones, M. (2014) *Doing Your Education Research Project*, 2nd edn. London: Sage.

Carrington, S., MacArthur, J., Kearney, A., Kimber, M., Mercer, L., Morton, M. and Rutherford, G. (2016) Towards an inclusive education for all, in S. Carrington and L. Carrington (eds) *Teaching in Inclusive School Communities*. Milton (Australia): Wiley. pp. 4–38.

Check, J. and Schutt, R.K. (2011) *Research Methods in Education*. London: Sage.

Clark A. (2004) The Mosaic approach and research with young children, in V. Lewis, M. Kellett, C. Robinson, S. Fraser and S. Ding (eds) *The Reality of Research with Children and Young People*. London: Sage. pp. 142–61.

Clark, A. (2011) Multimodal map making with young children: Exploring ethnographic and participatory methods. *Qualitative Research*, 11(3): 311–30.

Clark, A. and Moss, P. (2011) *Listening to Young Children: The Mosaic Approach*, 2nd edn. London: National Children's Bureau.

Clay, M. (2019) *An Observation Survey of Early Literacy Achievement*, 4th edn. Portsmouth, NH: Heinemann.

Cohen, L., Manion, L. and Morrison, K. (2018) *Research Methods in Education*, 8th edn. London: Routledge.

Crotty, M. (1998) *The Foundations of Social Research*. London: Sage.

Cuskelly, M. (2005) Ethical inclusion of children with disabilities in research, in A. Farrell (ed.) *Ethical Research with Children*. Maidenhead: Open University Press. pp. 97–111.

Danaher, G., Schirato, T. and Webb, J. (2000) *Understanding Foucault*. London: Sage.

Davis, J. and Watson, N. (2017) Disabled children, ethnography and unspoken understandings: The collaborative construction of diverse identities, in P. Christensen and A. James (eds) *Research with Children: Perspectives and Practices*, 3rd edn. London: Routledge. pp. 121–41.

de Bruin, C. (2017) Conceptualizing effectiveness in disability research. *International Journal of Research and Method in Education*, 40(2): 113–36.

Deer, B. (2011) How the case against the MMR vaccine was fixed. *British Medical Journal*, 342. www.bmj.com/content/342/bmj.c5347

Denzin, N. and Lincoln, Y. (2012) *Strategies of Qualitative Inquiry*. London: Sage.

Department for Education (DfE) (2014) *The National Curriculum in England: Complete Framework for Key Stages 1 to 4*. www.gov.uk/government/publications/national-curriculum-in-england-framework-for-key-stages-1-to-4

Department for Education (DfE) (2019) Permanent and fixed period exclusions in England 2017–2018. Statistical release. www.gov.uk/government/statistics/permanent-and-fixed-period-exclusions-in-england-2017-to-2018

Department for Education (DfE) and Department of Health (DH) (2015) *Special Educational Needs and Disability Code of Practice: 0 to 25 years*. https://assets.publishing.service.gov.uk/government/uploads/system/uploads/attachment_data/file/398815/SEND_Code_of_Practice_January_2015.pdf

Dunne, L., Hallett, F., Kay, V. and Woolhouse, V. (2018) Spaces of inclusion investigating place, positioning and perspective in educational settings through photo-elicitation. *International Journal of Inclusive Education*, 22(1): 21–37.

Durcikova, A., Lee, A.S. and Brown, S.A. (2018) Making rigorous research relevant: Innovating statistical action research. *MIS Quarterly*, 42(1): 241–63.

Fayette, R. and Bond, C. (2017) A systematic literature review of qualitative research methods for eliciting the views of young people with ASD about their educational experiences. *European Journal of Special Needs Education*, 33(3): 349–65.

Florian, L. and Black-Hawkins, K. (2011) Exploring inclusive pedagogy. *British Educational Research Journal*, 37(5): 813–28.

Flyvbjerg, B. (2006) Five misunderstandings about case-study research. *Qualitative Inquiry*, 12(2): 219–45.

Fosnot, C.T. (1989) *Enquiring Teachers, Enquiring Learners: A Constructivist Approach for Teaching*. New York: Teachers College Press.

Giangreco, M., Cater, E., Doyle, M.B. and Suter, J. (2010) Supporting students with disabilities in inclusive classrooms, in R. Rose (ed.), *Confronting Obstacles to Inclusion*. London: Routledge. pp. 248–63.

Glaser, B.G. (1965) The constant comparative method of qualitative analysis. *Social Problems*, 12(4): 436–45.

Graham, A., Powell, M., Taylor, N., Anderson, D. and Fitzgerald, R. (2013) *Ethical Research Involving Children*. Florence: UNICEF Office of Research-Innocenti.

Gray, C. and Winter, E. (2011) Hearing voices: Participatory research with preschool children with and without disabilities. *European Early Childhood Education Research Journal*, 21(3): 231–33.

Guba, E.G. and Lincoln, Y.S. (1994) Competing paradigms in qualitative research, in N.K. Denzin and Y.S. Lincoln (eds), *Handbook of Qualitative Research*. London: Sage. pp.105–17.

Hammersley, M. (1985) From ethnography to theory: A programme and paradigm in the sociology of education. *Sociology*, 19(2): 244–59.

Harcourt, D. (2011) An encounter with children: Seeking meaning and understanding about childhood. *European Early Childhood Education Research Journal*, 19(3): 331–43.

Harcourt, D. and Einarsdóttir, J. (2011) Introducing children's perspectives and participation in research. *European Early Childhood Education Research Journal*, 19(3): 301–7.

Harrowell, I., Hollén, L., Lingam, R. and Emond, A. (2018) The impact of developmental coordination disorder on educational achievement in secondary school. *Research in Developmental Disabilities*, 72: 13–22.

Hart, R. (1997) *Children's Participation*. London: UNICEF and Earthscan.

Hill, L. (2014) 'Some of it I haven't told anybody else': Using photo elicitation to explore the experiences of secondary school education from the perspective of young people with a diagnosis of autistic spectrum disorder. *Educational & Child Psychology*, 31(1): 79–89.

Hodkinson, A. (2015) *Key Issues in Special Educational Needs and Inclusion*. London: Sage.

Keegan, R. (2016) Action research as an agent for enhancing teaching and learning in physical education: A physical education teacher's perspective. *The Physical Educator*, 73(2): 225–84.

Kellett, M. (2005) *Children as active researchers: A new research paradigm for the 21st century?* ESRC National Centre for Research Methods, University of Southampton.

Kellett, M. (2010) *Rethinking Children and Research: Attitudes in Contemporary Society.* London: Continuum.

Kiernan, C. (1999) Participation in research by people with learning difficulties: Origins and issues. *British Journal of Learning Disabilities*, 27: 43–7.

Kirylo, J.D. (2020) *Reinventing the Pedagogy of the Oppressed: Contemporary Critical Perspectives.* London: Bloomsbury.

Kumar, R. (2018) *Research Methodology: A Step-by-Step Guide for Beginners.* London: Sage.

Lambert, M. (2012) *A Beginner's Guide to Doing Your Education Research Project.* London: Sage.

Lomax, H. (2012) Contested voices? Methodological tensions in creative visual research with children. *International Journal of Social Research Methodology*, 15(2): 105–17.

MacLeod, A., Lewis, A. and Robertson, C. (2014) 'CHARLIE: PLEASE RESPOND!' Using participatory methodology with individuals on the autism spectrum. *International Journal of Research and Method in Education*, 37(4): 407–20.

MacNaughton, G. and Smith, K. (2005) Transforming research ethics: The choices and challenges of researching with children, in A. Farrell (ed.), *Ethical Research with Children*. Maidenhead: Open University Press. pp. 112–23.

Mayne, F., Howitt, C. and Rennie, L. (2017) Using interactive nonfiction narrative to enhance competence in the informed consent process with 3-year-old children. *International Journal of Inclusive Education*, 21(3): 299–315.

Messiou, K. (2016) Research in the field of inclusive education: Time for a rethink? *International Journal of Inclusive Education*, 21(2): 146–59.

Mortari, L. and Harcourt, D. (2012) 'Living' ethical dilemmas for researchers when researching with children. *International Journal of Early Years Education*, 20(3): 234–43.

Mouly, G. (1978) *Education Research: The Art and Science of Investigation.* Boston: Allyn and Bacon.

Mukherji, P. and Albon, D. (2015) *Research Methods in Early Childhood: An Introductory Guide.* London: Sage.

Murray, J. (2017) Welcome in! How the academy can warrant recognition of young children as researchers. *European Early Childhood Education Research Journal*, 25(2): 224–42.

Mutch, C. (2013) *Doing Educational Research: A Practitioner's Guide to Getting Started.* Wellington (NZ): New Zealand Council of Educational Research.

Oakley, A. (1981) Interviewing women: A contradiction in terms, in H. Roberts (ed.), *Doing Feminist Research*. London: Routledge. pp. 30–61.

Opie, J., Deppeler, J. and Southcott, J. (2017) 'You have to be like everyone else': Support for students with vision impairment in mainstream secondary schools. *Support for Learning*, 32(3): 267–87.

Palaiologou, I. (2019) *Child Observation. A Guide for Students of Early Childhood*, 4th edn. London: Sage.

Pimlott-Wilson, H. (2012) Visualising children's participation in research: Lego Duplo, rainbows and clouds and moodboards. *International Journal of Social Research Methodology*, 15(2): 135–48.

Punch, S. (2009) Case study: Researching childhoods in rural Bolivia, in E. Kay M. Tisdall, J. Davis and M. Gallagher (eds) *Researching with Children and Young People*. London: Sage. pp. 89–96.

Reed-Danahay, D. (2017) Bourdieu and critical autoethnography: Implications for research, writing, and teaching. *International Journal of Multicultural Education*, 19(1): 144–54.

Robert-Holmes, G. (2011) *Doing Your Early Years Research Project*, 2nd edn. London: Sage.

Roberts, P. (2018) Theory as research: Philosophical work in education, in J. Quay, J. Bleasby, S. Stolz, M. Toscano and S. Webster (eds), *Philosophy in Educational Research: Methodological Dialogues*. London: Routledge.

Robson, C. (2002) *Real World Research: A Resource for Social Scientists and Practitioner-Researchers*. London: John Wiley & Sons.

Saddler, H. (2014) Researching the influence of teaching assistants on the learning of pupils identified with special educational needs in mainstream primary schools: Exploring social inclusion. *Journal of Research in Special Educational Needs*, 14: 145–52.

Sartori, G. (1970) Concept misformation in comparative politics. *The American Political Science Review*, 64(4): 1033–53.

Scotland, J. (2012) Exploring the philosophical underpinnings of research: Relating ontology and epistemology to the methodology and methods of the scientific, interpretive, and critical research paradigms. *English Language Teaching*, 5(9): 9–16.

Scott, P., Haworth, J., Conrad, C. and Neumann, A. (1993) Notes on the classroom as field setting: Learning and teaching qualitative research in higher education. *Qualitative Research in Higher Education*, 3(6): 3–24.

Scott-Barrett, J., Cebula, K. and Florian, L. (2019) Listening to young people with autism: Learning from researcher experience. *International Journal of Research and Method in Education*, 42(2): 163–84.

Sharples, J., Webster, R. and Blatchford. P. (2015) *Making Best Use of Teaching Assistants*. London: Education Endowment Fund.

Simons, H. (2009) *Case Study Research in Practice*. London: Sage.

Tashakkori, A. and Teddlie, C. (2003) The past and future of mixed methods research: From data triangulation to mixed model designs, in A. Tashakkori and C. Teddlie (eds), *Handbook of Mixed Methods in Social and Behavioral Research*. London: Sage. pp. 671–701.

Thomas, G. (2017) *How to Do Your Research Project: A Guide for Students*. London: Sage.

Thomson, P. (2020) *Patter* (blog) https://patthomson.net/2014/06/09/aims-and-objectives-whats-the-difference

UNCRC (1989) Convention on the Rights of the Child. *UN General Assembly Resolution 44/25*. www.ohchr.org/en/professionalinterest/pages/crc.aspx

Vygotsky, L.S. (1978) *Mind in Society: The Development of Higher Psychological Processes*. London: Harvard University Press.

Wall, K. (2017) Exploring the ethical issues related to visual methodology when including young children's voice in wider research samples. *International Journal of Inclusive Education*, 21(3): 316–31.

Walliman, N. (2006) *Social Research Methods*. London: Sage.

World Medical Association (1954) *Principles for Those in Research and Experimentation*. Fernay-Voltaire: WMA.

Wragg, E. (2012) *An Introduction to Classroom Observation*. London: Routledge.

Yin, R.K. (2018) *Case Study Research and Applications*. London: Sage.

INDEX